ENTERPRISE RESOURCE PLANNING

Nirupma Pathak
HOD, Department of Computer Application,
Lal Bahadur Shastri Girls College of Management (LBSGCM),
Lucknow.

Sanchita Ghatak
Senior Lecturer.
Jaipuria Institute of Management,
Lucknow.

Satyendra K Singh
HOD, Internet Institute for
Special Education, Lucknow.

Himalaya Publishing House

MUMBAI • NEW DELHI • NAGPUR • BENGALURU • HYDERABAD • CHENNAI • PUNE • LUCKNOW • AHMEDABAD • ERNAKULAM • BHUBANESWAR • INDORE • KOLKATA • GUWAHATI

First Edition : 2012

Published by : Mrs. Meena Pandey for **Himalaya Publishing House Pvt. Ltd.,** "Ramdoot", Dr. Bhalerao Marg, Girgaon, **Mumbai - 400 004.** Phone: 022-23860170/23863863, Fax: 022-23877178 **E-mail: himpub@vsnl.com; Website: www.himpub.com**

Branch Offices :

New Delhi : "Pooja Apartments", 4-B, Murari Lal Street, Ansari Road, Darya Ganj, New Delhi - 110 002. Phone: 011-23270392, 23278631; Fax: 011-23256286

Nagpur : Kundanlal Chandak Industrial Estate, Ghat Road, Nagpur - 440 018. Phone: 0712-2738731, 3296733; Telefax: 0712-2721215

Bengaluru : No. 16/1 (Old 12/1), 1st Floor, Next to Hotel Highlands, Madhava Nagar, Race Course Road, Bengaluru - 560 001. Phone: 080-32919385; Telefax: 080-22286611

Hyderabad : No. 3-4-184, Lingampally, Besides Raghavendra Swamy Matham, Kachiguda, Hyderabad - 500 027. Phone: 040-27560041, 27550139; Mobile: 09390905282

Chennai : No. 8/2, Modley 2nd Street, Ground Floor, T. Nagar, Chennai - 600 017. Phone: 044-28144004/28144005; Mobile: 09345345051

Pune : First Floor, "Laksha" Apartment, No. 527, Mehunpura, Shaniwarpeth (Near Prabhat Theatre), Pune - 411 030. Phone: 020-24496323/24496333; Mobile: 09370579333

Lucknow : Jai Baba Bhavan, Church Road, Near Manas Complex and Dr. Awasthi Clinic, Aliganj, Lucknow - 226 024 (U.P.). Phone: 0522-2339329, 4068914; Mobile: 09307501550

Ahmedabad : 114, "SHAIL", 1st Floor, Opp. Madhu Sudan House, C.G. Road, Navrang Pura, Ahmedabad - 380 009. Phone: 079-26560126; Mobile: 09377088847

Ernakulam : 39/104 A, Lakshmi Apartment, Karikkamuri Cross Rd., Ernakulam, Cochin - 622011, Kerala. Phone: 0484-2378012, 2378016; Mobile: 09344199799

Bhubaneswar : 5 Station Square, Bhubaneswar - 751 001 (Odisha). Phone: 0674-2532129, Mobile: 09338746007

Indore : Kesardeep Avenue Extension, 73, Narayan Bagh, Flat No. 302, IIIrd Floor, Near Humpty Dumpty School, Indore - 452 007 (M.P.). Mobile: 09301386468

Kolkata : 108/4, Beliaghata Main Road, Near ID Hospital, Opp. SBI Bank, Kolkata - 700 010, Phone: 033-32449649, Mobile: 09910440956

Guwahati : House No. 15, Behind Pragjyotish College, Near Sharma Printing Press, P.O. Bharalumukh, Guwahati - 781009, (Assam). Mobile: 09883055590, 09883055536

DTP by : Bright Computer Systems, Gayatri Nagar, Sitapur Road, Lucknow Mobile: 9450614766, 9793630385

Printed at : A to Z Printers, New Delhi. On behalf of HPH.

PREFACE

The primary objective of the book "Enterprise Resource Planning" is to introduce the students of computer science with various issues of Information sharing, usage and dissemination and expose them to the concepts of Enterprise Resource Planning (ERP). ERP systems integrate the information across the functions of the organization such as accounting, finance, marketing, production, and human resource development. It also embeds the organizational processes leading to process discipline. Backed with integrated information systems and tightly integrated processes, ERP effectively support managerial decision-making. The ERP backbone creates a supporting backbone for enterprise application(s) integration

This book aims to highlight the integration of business processes and computer applications across business functions and also demonstrates how organizations are represented in an ERP system and features of such software packages (from managerial and technical perspective) very broadly. Thus this edition of the book shows a well organized contents of the subject Enterprise Resource Planning as per the syllabus of various universities in India as well as abroad.

The author hopes that the book will fulfill the need of readers and would welcome any suggestions towards the improvement of the book.

Authors

ACKNOWLEDGEMENT

I am extremely thankful to our dear students as the interaction with them helped us in understanding their needs.

I extend our heartiest thanks to all the authors whose research works and books were referred while preparing the content of this book.

I thank Dr. Sunil Kumar (Director), LBSIMDS, Lucknow as he has been a source of inspiration for such creative work and initiatives.

Our heartfelt gratitude to Dr. Subhash Chandra (Director) MLRSM, Lucknow, Mr. Anshum Srivastava, HOD, LBSIMDS and Dr. Syed Haider Ali, Director, Goel Group of Institutes. Special thanks to Ms. Natasha Kanojia and Ms Sonali Kanojia who helped in drafting the contents with their insights.

I am sincerely grateful to my family, specially my parents Mrs. Bindeshwari Devi Pathak and Mr. Devi Prasad Pathak, beloved Brothers Abhishek Pathak (DBA), Mirzapur, Akhilesh Pathak (Income Tax Officer), NIC, Allahabad, Ashutosh Pathak and Ashish Pathak, Sisters Anupama Pathak, Archana Pathak and Rachana Pathak for their good wishes, love moral support and vocal on encouragement and without them this manuscript would not have been completed successfully. I also gratify them for abiding me ever and anon to come to grips with all ups and downs of life.

I deeply express my heartfelt thanks to Himalaya Publishing House, New Delhi for publishing this book in such. A beautiful get up and well in time last but not the least, all praise, laud and honor to great Almighty God for His amazing grace and Guidance.

Nirupma Pathak

nirupmapathak@gmail.com

I thank Sai Baba for his blessings which made me complete this book. My love and appreciation to my son Snigdh who was always cooperative. My sincere thanks to HPH for their support in bringing out this book in such a short span of time.

Sanchita Ghatak

I extend my special thanks to my family and my colleagues who have always been motivating me to come with this book.

I appreciate the opportunity given by Mr M.C. Pandey from Himalaya Publishing House to start and complete this project.

(Satyendra K Singh)

CONTENTS

1 ERP Introduction

Introduction

In an industry where competition is intense and changes have been dramatic, the information technology has raised the standard of living and the way to do business. Information technology is spreading like a forest fire as compared to the conventional personal computer which was more like a type writer but currently users have become very demanding as a result IT has found a vast scope in its usage pattern.

Organizations are using this technology (IT) for strategic, managerial and operational activities involved in the gathering, processing, storing, distributing and use of information, which we term as Information System (IS).

Information System

There are various units of information systems, for example: transaction processing systems, office systems, decision support systems, knowledge management systems, database management systems, and office information systems. Critical to most information systems are information technologies, which are typically designed to enable humans to perform tasks for which the human brain is not well suited, such as: handling large amounts of information, performing complex calculations, and controlling many simultaneous processes.

Some examples of such systems are:

- Data warehouses
- Enterprise resource planning
- Enterprise systems

- Expert systems
- Geographic information system
- Global information system
- Office Automation

In recent times, many organizations have initiated Enterprise Resource Planning (ERP) systems. The market of ERP has been one of the fastest growing markets in the software industry. ERP system support the major functional areas of the business including sales order processing, purchasing, production planning, financial accounting, management accounting, and human resources.

The word ERP has revolutionized across the world and it has been widely used in IT magazine, seminaries and companies. Concepts relevant to ERP are concisely discussed below:

Enterprise

Enterprise is defined as a team of people working to acquire and transform resource with a common goal.

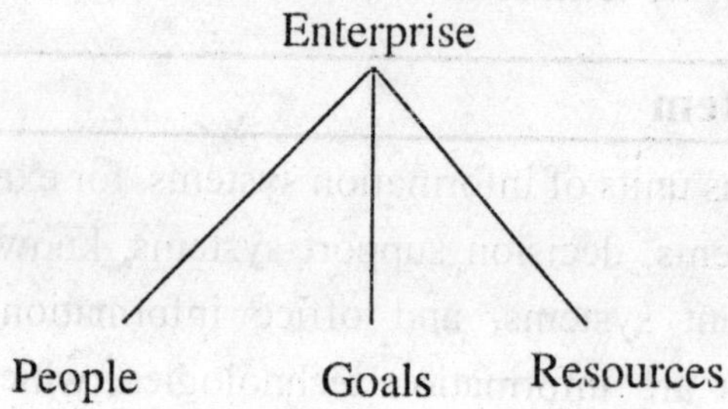

Fig. 1.1

The Enterprise behaves as a single entity with a growing a venture.

Communication pattern between departments

In the traditional approach, the organizations were divided into different units based on the functions they performed, and each unit though being a part of the organization, were solitary in functioning, as shown below.

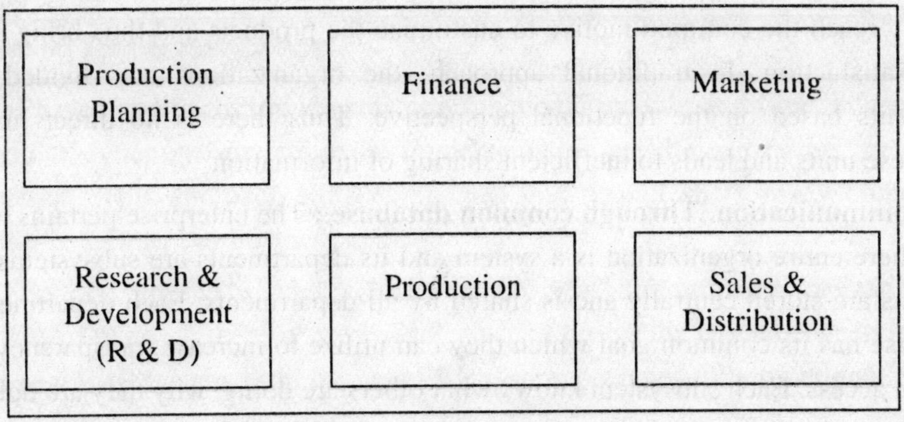

Fig. 1.2

There need to be a system by which all these units of the organization should be able to communicate, and disseminate data information amongst themselves. The communication or information sharing can be done by following models.

(*a*) No or little communication between departments: Organizations are divided into departments. The departments are as follows:

(*i*) Production Department.

(*ii*) Production Planning Department

(*iii*) Finance Department.

(*iv*) Sales And Distribution Department

(*v*) Purchasing Department

(*vi*) R & D Department Etc.

Earlier all these departments work in isolation. The data generated in of these departments could be communicated only to the top management. Thus due to lack of synchronization the departments diverts from a common organization goal and hence they end up pulling it in different directions and also, sometimes the departmental objectives become conflicting. For instance Today's customer want more variety in products, so to satisfy the customer's need, the sales and marketing departments will want product variety, but the production department want to limit the product variety to cut down production costs, hence due to lack of information sharing about demand and production, coordination is not possible. Thus the organization will not be able to successfully reach the common motive to customize the products and thus bring about customer satisfaction. In traditional approach, the organizations are divided into different units based on the functional perspective. Thus there is no direct linkage between these units and leads to inefficient sharing of information.

(*b*) **Communication. Through common database :** The enterprise pertains to the division where entire organization is a system and its departments are subsystems. All informations are stored centrally and is shared by all departments. Each department in the enterprise has its common goal which they can utilize to increase transparency and information access. Each subsystem knows what others are doing, why they are doing it and what should be done to move the company towards the common goal.

Integrating various sections of the organizations so as to make them act as one unit is a necessary aspect in ERP implementation in the organization, which determines the smooth operations of the business enterprise and ensures appropriate co-ordination between various departments in the enterprise.

In such a system the information is stored in a common database and the various departments share that common information as is they all are working in a common platform..

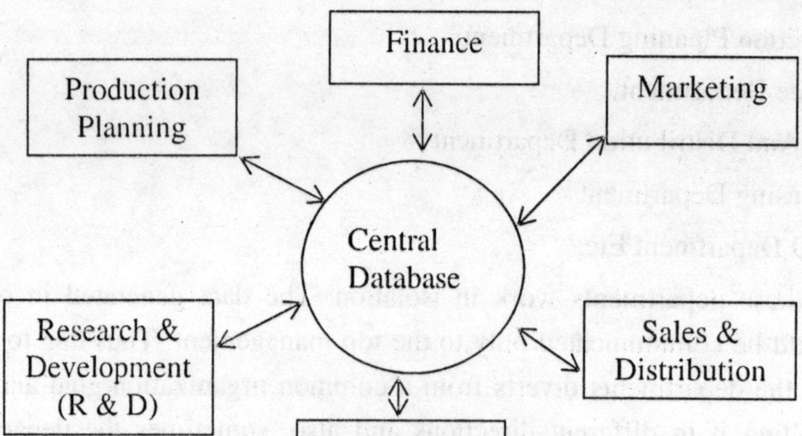

Fig. 1.3

Enterprise Resource Planning

ERP is most widely used approach in business software systems which are mostly implemented in industries and organization. ERP is the acronym of Enterprise Resource Planning. This system is an integration of both software and business strategies.

To ensure smooth performance of an organization, ERP implementation utilizes ERP software applications through resource planning, management, operational control.

ERP is supported by multi-module application software which integrates activities of functional units such as production planning, purchasing, inventory control, product distribution, order tracking etc.

Finance, accounting and human resource are some common business activities in an organization and ERP has separate module for all these units.

ERP Definition

ERP is a business management system that integrates all facades of the business, including planning, manufacturing, sales, and marketing. As ERP has become more common in the business world, software application modules have emerged to facilitate business activities across functional departments.

CRM (Customers Relationship Management) and SCM (Supply Chain Management) are the two most common enterprise software's designed to standardize the working of various organizations. The functionality of ERP envelops CRM and SCM. Where CRM collaborates with customers to enhance the relationship and SCM facilitate collaboration with the organization, suppliers, manufacturers distributors and the partners.

ERP – A System Perspective

ERP, often like other IT and business concept can be defined in many different ways. According to system theory ERP has its goal, components and boundary, which are as follows:

Goal

The goal of ERP is to grow-up as a full-fledged and improved in internal business processes by adopting renovation and initiating re-engineering strategies in current business processes.

Component of an ERP System

The component of Management Information System and ERP reasonable broadly with each other as discussed below:

- **ERP Software:** Module based ERP software is the core of an ERP system. The conventional ER software module accelerates the efficiency of a functional area within an organization. Usually used ERP software modules include product planning, parts purchasing, inventory control, product distribution, order tracking, finance, accounting and human resources aspects of an organization.
- **Business Process:** Organization offers three levels in business processes strategic planning. To enable the easy support in business processes at all levels, ERP has been promoted. But transaction in ERP success may be configured or limited due to the integration of various functional departments.
- **ERP Users:** ERP system is accessed by the all levels of employees in the organization such as from workers, supervisors, mid-level managers to executive.
- **Hardware and Operating System:** Legacy ERP systems may use any Operating system(O.S), but now ERP systems operates mostly with Unix O.S. Windows NT and Linux are other O.S. which are popularly used to run ERP software's
- **The Boundary of an ERP System:** The organization boundary is more wider than the boundary of an ERP system which in contrast to the boundary of supply chain system and e-commerce system that extends to the organization's suppliers, distributors, partners and customers. However ERP implementation should be broadened by involving the integration of ERP with external information system.

ERP System

An ERP System is an association of ERP software, business processes, users and hardware that run the ERP software. An ERP is such more than just a computer software and an ERP system is more than the sum of its parts or components. Stream line and improve organization's business processes is the common goal of such components into which intelligent users play the effective role because any standard

ERP software would consist hundreds of input information foray particular business activity. To take advantage of ERP software, skilled and dynamic knowledge of each entity of system is necessary.

ERP Software

To upgrade the level of an organization, the ERP modules should be implemented as ERP software applications which automatics business processes within a functional department major ERP software modules cover the major functional areas of organization few common ERP modules are as follows:

(1) Product Planning Module (2) Parts And Material Purchasing Module (3) Inventory Control Module (4) Product Distribution Module (5) Order Tracing Module (6) Finance Module (7) Accounting Module (8) Marketing Module (9) HR Module.

Re-engineering of Business Processes

An organizational process involves three levels- strategic planning, management control and operational control. ERP success lays down in facilitating operational co-ordination across departments as to streamline and automatic entry rise wide resource planning at strategic planning level. Due to convention calls for the integration of ERP with other enterprise applications and demand long term management commitment into which the succors of ERP at strategic planning management control depends.

ERP Users

The users of an ERP system include workers and employees from all levels of an organization. Following Anthony R.A.'s classification of organizational processes workers can be classified into (1) those who execute strategic planning (2) those who perform managerial work (3) those who do operational work

Operating Systems for ERP

ERP software works on various O.S. like Unix or Windows and hardware like main frame. Organization may acquire the ERP and other enterprise software from any vendor in market, but the basic requirements for running. ERP application are-

(1) Security

(2) Stability

(3) Scalability, and

(4) Open standards.

Evolution of ERP

ERP evolves from MRP (Manufacturing Requirement Planning II) in 1980s, associated primarily to manufacturing industry and was designed to control manufacturing processes and planning the desired production with efficient output as an ultimate goal of an industry, whereas MRP itself has originated from inventory management & control in 1960s, designed mainly with an objective for management of stocks. From business perspective ERP has shown huge expansion from co-ordination of manufacturing processes to the integration of enterprise wide backend processes like production planning, scheduling and delivery. In technological field, ERP has upgraded itself from legacy implementation to more flexible tired client server architecture. The following table summarizes the evolution of ERP from 1960s to 1990s.

Timeline	System	Description
1960s	Control	The collaboration of information technology and business process of maintaining the appropriate level of stock in a warehouse leads to inventory management control. The activities of inventory management include identifying inventory requirement, setting targets, providing replenishment techniques and options, monitoring item usage, reconciling the inventory balances and reporting inventory status.
1970s	MRP	MRP essentially includes software applications for scheduling production processes. MRP effectively generates schedules or step-by-step approach method for the operations and raw material purchases based on the production requirement of finished goods, structure of the production system, the current inventory level and the lot sizing procedure for each operation.
1980s	MRP II	MRP utilizes software application. for coordinating manufacturing processes from product planning, parts

		purchasing, inventory control for product distribution.
1990s	ERP	ERP utilizes multi-module application software for enhancing the functioning of the internal business processes. ERP systems integrates business activities across functional departments, from product planning, parts purchasing, inventory control, product distribution, fulfillment to order tracking, ERP software system may include application modules for supporting marketing, finance, accounting, and human resources.

Benefits of ERP

ERP integrates the whole business, its departments and various tasks heads as an unified enterprise. The major benefits of ERP are improved co-ordination across functional departments, increased efficiencies of doing business and to facilitate day-to-day management.

ERP systems greatly respond to streamline the business processes. For the goodwill of ERP system, Organizations need to make sure that they have their information in line which helps to make the process swift. ERP doesn't bother about what the company deals with; it just depends on the company, with the right system and performance. ERP minimizes the operating cost It assembles and co-ordinates the company's process and streamlines processes where everything can be accessed through one enterprise wide information network.

Reduction in operating cost automatically leads to control of inventory, production, and marketing costs, and also helps to lower desk support. The establishment of backbone for data warehouses is supported by ERP and allows employees to access the information in real time, which in turn helps with research decision making and managerial control. It tracks actual cost of the daily activities and can perform activity or function based on costing.

Though, resource planning is the toughest process but ERP supports resource planning in the strategic planning process, which has proved to be beneficial in handling this traditional problem. The functionality that ERP system provides can help employees work through the strategy planning sessions and develop a comprehensive outlook that will aid in the company's processes.

The standard quality and design of ERP programs are always updated and renovated. In order to ensure quality control in the organization different ERP packages are available in the market but the company should make sure that they approach and try out the best one on the bases of diligence. Several programs even offer mobile capabilities to do the work anytime and anywhere.

ERP system is backed up strongly with real time capabilities which enable us to view and work with the recent updates in the company. With ERP system, the business will not only never suffer inventory shortages or wastages but also ensure the timely delivery of files done. An ERP system should be analyzed before purchasing and derive a conclusion that how it will work with the business.

ERP systems have both direct & indirect advantages:-

Direct: The direct advantages include improved efficiency, information integration for better decision making, faster response time to customer queries etc.

Indirect: The indirect benefits include better corporate image, improved customer goodwill, customers' satisfaction & so on. As we have already seen, some of these are tangible benefits while others are intangible. Now we will discuss some of the tangible and intangible benefits of ERP .

According to a survey of the Deloitte consulting, the **tangible benefits** of ERP are Inventory Reduction, Personal cost Reduction, Productivity Improvements, Close cycle reduction, and Financial and other management improvements.

However **intangible benefits** of ERP are Information visibility new improved process customer responsiveness cost reduction, Integration standardization flexibility globalization, and Technology business performance supply demand chain.

Now we will discuss in details about some of the tangible and intangible benefits of the ERP systems, they are—

- Information Integration
- Reduction of lead time
- On time shipment
- Cycle time Reduction

- Better customer satisfaction
- Reduced quality cost
- Improved information accuracy & decision making capability.
- Use of latest technology

Information Integration: One of the main and direct advantages lies in the promotion of integration. And the reason why ERP system is called integrated system is that they have the capability to automatically update data between related business functions and components. For instance, if only the status of an order at one place is updated, then in the order processing system all the other components will automatically get updated.

Reduction of lead time: The time taken between the order placement and the final delivery of the product is known as the lead time. The lead time for a good ERP system should be reduced which plays a important role in purchase and inventory control department. All this can happen by adopting the latest technologies such as electronic fund transfer (EFT) and electronic data interchange (EDI).

On Time Shipment: Companies offers the flexibility to deliver customer specific products with the lead time of standard, off the shelf product, when being customized or mode of production being changed as per order, its time and cost are considered and computed carefully. ERP system provides the freedom to change manufacturing and planning methods, as needs change without modifying the workplace.

Cycle Time Reduction: Cycle time is the time between receiving the order and delivery of order. Reduction will be more if the time gap between order and delivery time is minimum.

Better customer satisfaction: One of the main advantages of ERP system is to ensure customer satisfaction through the better supply of products and services.

Reduced Quality Cost: There are different ways the quality can be defined it can be excellence, confirmation to standards, fitness in price value etc. The American society for quality control (AQC) provides standard for quality management of costs on several quality masters. Operations managers have found the classification system useful for collecting data that are consistent and for identifying the opportunities in controlling quality cost which will show the immediate effect on efficiency.

Improve information accuracy & decision making capabilities:

(*a*) In order to manage the information.

(*b*) In order to deliver high quality information to the decision maker at right time.

(*c*) In order to process the data collection accurately.

All the above mentioned facts can be effectively performed if the organization adopts the best way to handle it.

Use of latest technologies: Another important advantage is the utilization of the latest development in IT. ERP quickly adapts themselves to take advantage of the latest technologies such as open system, c/s system, and the internet/intranet.

(*a*) **Operational Control, Management Control, Strategic Planning:** According to Anthony, R.A. – Strategic planning, management control and operational control are the three levels in which organizational processes ERP fall into success has benefited the operational co-ordination across functional areas. Strategic planning and management control will get the benefit if the ERP systems is successfully implemented.

(*b*) **Help Reduce Operating Costs:** ERP attempts to integrate business processes across the departments into a single enterprise wide information system. Through ERP we get following benefits.

(1) It improves co-ordination across functional departments.

(2) It increased efficiency for doing business.

(3) Reduced operating costs is the immediate benefit we get from implementing ERP system, and these reduced operating costs include lower inventory control cost, lower production cost, lower marketing cost and lower help desk support cost.

(*c*) **Facilitate Day-to-Day Management:** Day-to-day management is another benefit we derive from ERP system. The implementation of ERP systems introduces the establishment of backbone data warehouses and offers better accessibility to data, so that management can have up-to-the minute access to information for decision making and managerial control. ERP software helps to track the actual costs of activities and perform activity based on costing.

(*d*) **Support Strategic Planning:** Strategic planning is a deliberate steps that needs resources, define a target audience and set of goals and objective, plan and design, coordinated strategies with evidence of success. We need to logically connect these strategies to needs, assets and desired outcomes, and at last measure and evaluate the process by outcomes.

Issues related with ERP implementation

(*a*) **Integration:** One to main focus of ERP is integration of data across departments. If the daily requirements of people are not taken care by ERP software, then the efficiency of individual suffers by implementing ERP. The big question that arises with ERP is whether the benefit of integration and collaboration can make up for the loss in personal efficiency or not.

(*b*) **Efficiency:** Another aim of ERP implementation is minimizing data redundancy and redundant data entry. Companies where integration is not considered as necessary will face a problem. ERP joins the users and allows them to work in collaboration, but not increase individual efficiency as such.

(*c*) **Cost Reduction:** The cost will be reduced only when company takes accounting and reporting seriously even before implementation and have to put a lot of manual effort to acquire it. But no cost will be reduced if they only fulfill mandatory statements and neglect the need of internal reporting in financial matters.

(*d*) **Accuracy:** It is considered that people are more accurate than software. The efforts of hard-working people should make their output accurate.

Disadvantages

(*a*) **Expensive:** ERP system sets a very high cost by involving software hardware implementation consultants, trainers, programmers, employees and business advisor from an outside source, to do all customization and end user training inside.

(*b*) **Not very flexible:** SAP has arranged itself to almost anything. In Navision one can develop almost anything in days which other software may not be capable of doing.

Reasons for the growth of the ERP Market

There is a great demand of ERP system in the market. Analysis of industry has analyzed that in the next 5 year the costing growth rates are going to be more than 30%.

The question arises is that why so many companies replacing their key business system. The reason being:

1. To enable improved business performance
   - Cycle time reduction
   - Inventory reduction
   - Order fulfillment improvement
2. To support business growth requirements
   - New products/product lines, new customers
   - Global requirements including multiple languages
3. To provide flexible, integrated, real time decision support.
   - Improve responsiveness across the organization.
4. To eliminate limitation in legacy systems
   - Fragmentation of data & processing
   - In supportable technologies

There are some of the reasons for growth late of ERP markets & ERP venders.

Why do Many Implementations Fail?

To accept transformation in implementation system is very difficult for many employees. The system fails if proper training is not provided to the employees. Another factor which lead to failure is the fear of unemployment. When procedure gets converted, people become surplus /redundant who were doing these jobs.

If the same employees are trained into a new system and works in more challenging environment it is good for them but even the best system fails if there is a resistance to change, so it is very important that the management should take the responsibility and necessary steps in advancing, training and removing the fears of their employees.

Why ERP Package being Used Raw

Difference between conventional application packages and ERP packages:

(1) ERP packages are multi taking as it handle individual business functions such as accounts and inventory along with entire range of business functions necessary for the company's operation.

(2) Largest organization and small business are targeted by ERP packages. They can be a constituent of a highly flexible decentralized database and through network an information system is connected.

(3) Due to globalization in companies and market share of manufacturing and selling, multi currency capacity has widened in the world as well as the management platforms has also to being hastened due to the global adaptation of enterprise information systems.

Integrated Management Information

Information systems are composed of 3 components people, procedure and data. The present day information s4ystems are arranged in combination set of people, hardware, software, communication network, and data resources.

MIS is also known as information reporting system which gives knowledge about various aspects that help management in decision making.

These systems have the integrated approach. There will be an accounting system for the finance department, production, planning system, manufacturing, inventory management system, and stores-management.

The essential characteristics of Management information system are as follows:

(1) Accuracy- Information has to be accurate.

(2) Relevancy – it must be relevant for decision maker

(3) Timelines – it must be available to decision maker when needed.

Business Modeling

One of the primary activities in ERP project is making of a business model. It is not only a mathematical model, but it represents business as one large system, sub-system and business processes connection and dependence on each other as shown in following figure.

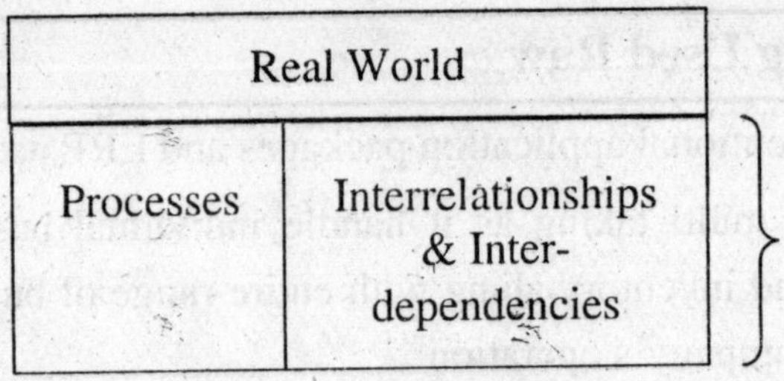

Real World & the Business Model

Fig. 1.4

Depending on the organization's goals, objectives, strategic plans and processes a business model is constructed.

Business model determines the ERP system to help various individual with the required information & necessary assistance so that they can perform their work were effectively, impressively and with full effort.

In short we can say that business model is a representation of the actual business – i.e., what are various business functions of the organization, how they related, what their interdependence are and so on.

Integrated Data Model

Making of an Integrated Data Model (IDM) is one of the difficult steps in ERP implementation. In the ERP system the advantage it provides is that the employees from different branch of administration get a way of approach to the data in an integrated manner. For detailed analysis and decision making company use this integrated data.

The things that we have to keep in mind while making plan for designing the data model for the ERP System is information integration & the process procedure automation.

REVIEW QUESTIONS

1. What is the critical factor that decides the success of an enterprise in today's competitive environment?
2. What is ERP?
3. Discuss the evolution of ERP?

4. What were the disadvantages of the pre-ERP information model the isolated islands model?
5. What are the advantages of ERP systems?
6. How is business integration achieved by ERP systems?
7. Why are ERP systems said to be flexible?
8. Why do many ERP implementations fail?
9. What are the reasons for the growth of the ERP market?
10. How do conventional application packages and ERP packages differ?
11. What is an enterprise?
12. What is an integrated information system?
13. Why are integrated information systems important for the organization's success?
14. What is business modeling?
15. What is an integrated date model?
16. What are the benefits of an EPP system?
17. What is lead time and how is it reduced by using an ERP system?
18. How does an ERP system reduce cycle time?
19. What are the intangible benefits of an ERP implementation?
20. How does an ERP system facilitate better decision making?

2 ERP AND RELATED TECHNOLOGIES

Introduction

ERP implementation involves special techniques and concepts for the integrated management of business as it leads to effective use of resources and to improve the efficiency of an enterprise.

ERP Limitations

- Success depends on the skill and experience of the workers; this includes training about how to make optimum use of the system.
- Companies employ new managers who lack knowledge about the company's ERP system, which creates a problem in handling the system till the time that person is not trained,
- ERP systems can be very expensive to implement, thus it involves a big implementation cost.
- ERP vendors charge an annual license renewal fee that is unrelated to the size of the company using it. This increases additional cost.
- Security is a big concern, for example when the company has to reveal the database structure to a developer, there may arise chances of data related security issue.
- The existing system may not be willing to reveal or share data amongst department, which is though a feature of ERP. This leads to a major problem in integration.

- Once a system is established, switching costs are very high.

To overcome the limitations of ERP system we have following technologies:

- Business Process Reengineering (BPR)
- Management Information System (MIS)
- Decision Support Systems (DSS)
- Executive Information Systems (EIS)
- Data warehousing(DATAWAREHOUSE)
- Data Mining(DM)
- On line Analytical Processing(OLAP)
- Product Life Cycle Management(PLM)
- Supply Chain Management (SCM)

Business Process Reengineering (BPR)

The abbreviation of BPR is business process reengineering. This is an important tool which makes organizations more efficient. This process leads to modernization and standardization of the organization. BPR formulates an organization in such a way that directly affects its performance.

Impact of BPR on Operation

The people and the processes are most important parameters of an organization i.e. both are complementary to each other. For e.g. if individuals are motivated and they work hard but activities of the business processes are cumbersome and non essential then it will lead into the poor performance of an organization. The success of BPR depends on transforming the process as to how people will work. What appears to be minor changes may have dramatic effects on cost flow, service delivery and customer satisfaction.

How to implement BPR Project

A top down design approach to map and improve the organizations, and avoid undertaking a project in isolation is the key to BPR success.

It means:

- Mission statement begins the project by defining the purpose of an organization and emphasizes by defining what makes it better from sectors and industry.

- Vision statements provides the organization a clear picture of the desired objective in future
- By constructing the structure of business strategy, it defines the project objective.
- Behavioral issue is also defined which will enable the organization to achieve its aim
- Key performance measures are produced to track the progress
- Efficiency advancement is associated to the culture of the organization
- To enhance the performance various initiatives required are identified.

One these building blocks in place, the BPR exercise can begin.

Tools to Support BPR

An organization where BPR projects are implemented should be capable of managing huge data, process & system. Thus if BPR fails to have an efficient and excellent tool then management of this information becomes very difficult. The adoption of good BPR documentation tool is a smart step taken in any BPR project.

The types of attributes you should look for in BPR software are:

- Graphical interface for fast documentation.
- Object oriented technology so that changes are automatically updated throughout the organization's procedures and documentation, if applied or done in one place.
- User friendly interface to have simplified step wise process.
- Meta data field is customizable or modifiable so that information related to industry, business sector; organization can be included and implemented.
- Quick maintenance and updating information in word document by touch of a single button in the website
- Analysis to show visually how responsibilities in a process are transferred between different roles, or where data items or computer applications are being used.
- Support for Value Stream mapping.
- CRUD or RACI reports, for providing evidences in process improvement.

- The ability to access the processes against agreed international standards
- Simulation software to support 'what-if' analyses during the design phase of the project to develop LEAN processes
- The production of word documents or web site versions of the procedures at the touch of a single button, so that the information can be easily maintained and updated.

Tools mainly responsible for bringing this change is IT when the importance of IT is understood by any BPR effort and adopting the pre-BPR analysis and planning phases despite considering other available IT options and thus the effort one IT solution which recommended by the employees and the organization is bound to clash during further proceeding or take off.

An ERP system implementation help in integrating the various business processes of the organization with the help of modern developments/advancements in IT sector. The goal of an organization to achieve dramatic improvements in sensitive areas such as cost, quality and speed etc. can be obtained with a good ERP package. ERP implementation sometimes limits or end many BPR initiatives.

Management Information System (MIS)

MIS effectively does the collection, transfer and presentation of information in the entire organization, by utilizing an integrated approach and information flow as its tool

Distinguishing features of MIS are as follows:

(1) As MIS work through the integrated database, it enables greater flexibility in meeting the information needs of the management.

(2) The MIS integrates the information among various functional areas such as accounting, marketing, manufacturing etc.

(3) Information is provided at all the level of management by MIS

The main **characteristics** of the MIS are

(1) The MIS supports the data processing functions of transaction handling & record keeping.

(2) MIS uses an integrated database and supports a variety of functional areas.

Decision Support System (DSS)

DSS allows two-way flow of information between user friendly integrated software & hardware tool and to the management that gets support to produce and present information targeted in decision making.

DSS fills the information gap and permits the manager to take smart decision in order to improve their quality. Thus to make this happen DSS hardware & software assigns the latest technological innovations an planning and forecasting models and 4th generation languages. They facilitate the work of decision making by developing alternative choices in decision making processes.

Decisions regarding the structured problems such as reorder of raw materials, how much to order is better supported by MIS but precision regarding semi-structured & unstructured problems are supported by DSS. Basically DSS is designed to supply the information to the managers in the way they want for e.g.-a manager wants to reduce cycle time and for that he might look at various aspect like the availability of raw materials, the average machine down time etc. so the manager's job becomes less repetitive in the system & hence DSS are capable of helping the managers in making such decision.

The main characteristics of a DSS are.

(1) A DSS is designed to address semi structured and unstructured problems.

(2) The DSS mainly supports decision making at the top management level.

(3) DSS is interactive, user friendly & independent from a computer professional to make decision.

(4) For decision makers DSS provides them general purpose models, simulation capabilities & analytical tools.

MIS Vs DSS

(1) Decisions regarding structured problems are supported by MIS but decisions regarding semi structured & unstructured problems are supported by DSS

(2) MIS focuses on various subjects planned reports but DSS focuses on its cause of making

(3) MIS is all time available in routine standard, scheduled and structured but DSS is available only on request and is unstructured

(4) Organization system is contained or compelled by MIS but DSS is quick, immediate & user friendly.

Executive Information System (EIS)

There is a very thin line that divides DSS & EIS. An EIS is a decision support system that is concerned with how decisions affect due to high pressure and problems faced by top level executives & decision makers. EIS is caters to these areas of concern. The following points are taken into consideration by EIS.

(1) The overall vision and mission of the company and the company goals.
(2) Strategic planning
(3) Organizational structure.
(4) Crisis management/contingency planning.
(5) Strategic control & monitoring of overall operations.
(6) The ultimate goal, mission and the vision of the company.

External information such as from the competitors, government regulations, trade group, new gathering agencies etc. is needed to access by executive decision makers but in such decisions a very high degree of uncertainty and future orientation is involved. EIS is easy to use and latest technological innovations make them flexible.

Data Warehousing (DATAWAREHOUSE)

A data warehouse is a platform to support many DSS and EIS application, and processes within an enterprise with the integrated data.

According to W.H. Inman, Data Warehouse (DATAWAREHOUSE) is defined as

"To support the management decisions, a DATAWAREHOUSE is a subject existed, integrated fine variant, non volatile collecting of data.

(OPS) Operational Data Store Vs. Data Warehouse (DATAWAREHOUSE)—

(1) OPS is volatile while DATAWAREHOUSE is permanent in nature
(2) OPS contains current data while DATAWAREHOUSE contain both current & legacy data.

Data Warehouse Components and Architecture

The incoming source of data in a data warehouse is from operational systems of the organization & external sources which collectively referred to as source systems.

The data extracted from source systems is processed, cleaned, transformed, combined, reduplicated to prepare the data for us in the data warehouse and is stored in a area called data staging area. Various machines combine to form the data staging area where simple activities like sorting and sequential processing takes place. But the activities like query and presentation is not undertaken by the data staging area, it undergoes and is categorized as a presentation server. The data free from the data staging area is organized stored and is loaded into a targeted machine of a presentation server for direct querying by end users, report writer & other applications.

DATAWAREHOUSE needs three different kinds of system such as:

1. Source Systems
2. Data Staging Area
3. Presentation servers

The three systems are cross linked with each other in such a way that the data travels from source system through the data staging area to the presentation servers. The entire process is popularly known as ETT (Extraction, Transformation, and Transportation). ETL (Extract, transform and load) tool is called DTS (Data Transformation Services) and Oracle's ETL tool is called OWB(Oracle Warehouse Builder) & MS server's.

A typical **architecture** of a data warehouse is shown below:

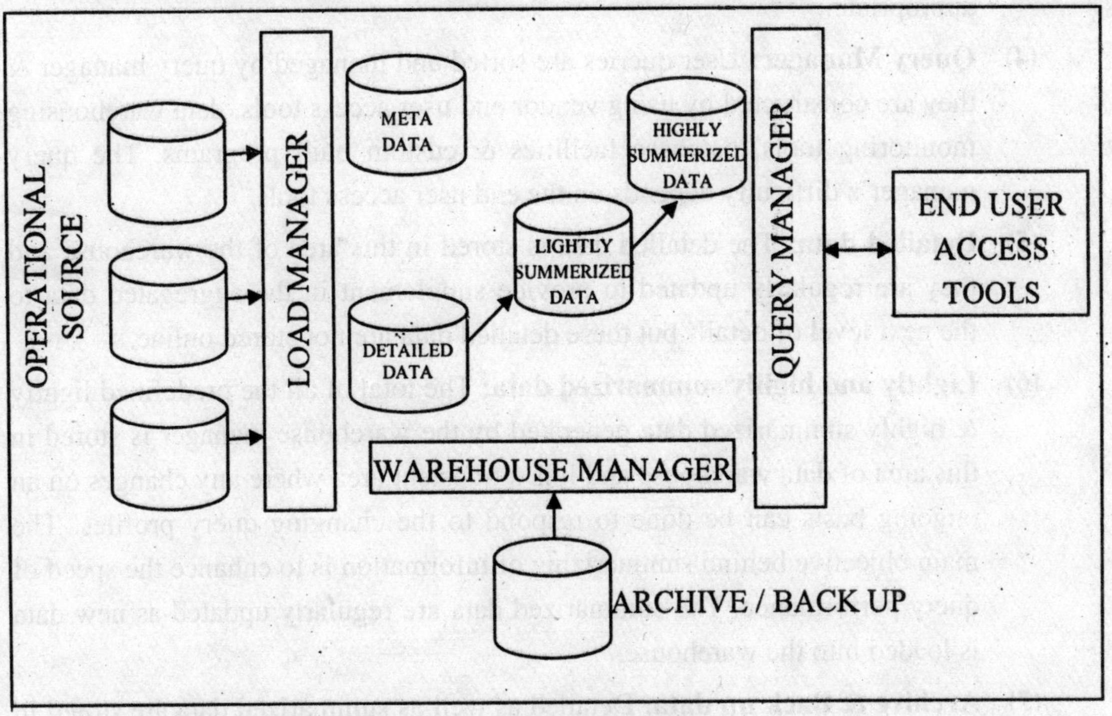

Components & their functions are explained below:

(1) **Operational Data:** In traditional network of mainframe system and hierarchical format it is one of the data sources. RDMS like oracle, Informix is also the source of data in DATAWAREHOUSE. Apart from these internal data sources, the operational data is also obtained from external sources such as commercial data and data associated with suppliers & customers.

(2) **Load Manager:** The operation related with extraction & loading data into the DATAWAREHOUSE is performed by the load manager to simplify the transformation of data for entry into the warehouse these operations are referred the size and complicity of load manager differs among various data warehouses and by using a combination of vendor data loading tools & custom built programs they can be constructed.

(3) **Warehouse Manager:** The management related operations in the data warehouse is performed by warehouse manager & they are constructed by using combination of vendor data management tool & custom built programs. According to the conditions, the warehouse manager also

generates query profiles to determine which index and aggregations are appropriate.

(4) **Query Manager:** User queries are sorted and managed by query manager & they are constructed by using vendor end user access tools, data warehousing monitoring tools, database facilities & custom built programs. The query manager's difficulty depends on the end user access tools.

(5) **Detailed data:** The detailed data is stored in this area of the warehouse and they are regularly updated to provide supplement in the aggregated data to the next level of details but these detailed data are not stored online.

(6) **Lightly and highly summarized data:** The total of all the predefined lightly & highly summarized data generated by the warehouse manager is stored in this area of data warehouse and it is a transient area where any changes on an ongoing basis can be done to respond to the changing query profiles. The main objective behind summarizing of information is to enhance the speed of query performance. The summarized data are regularly updated as new data is loaded into the warehouse.

(7) **Archive & Back up data:** Detailed as well as summarized data are stored in this area of warehouse for the purpose of achieving and backup, the stored data is transferred to storage achieve devices such as magnetic tapes & optical disks.

(8) **Metadata:** Metadata (data about data) is stored in DATAWAREHOUSE and its definition is used by all processes in the warehouse. It is used for variety of purposes such as

(*i*) The extraction & loading process: Mapping of data sources having a common view of information within the warehouse is done by metadata.

(*ii*) The warehouse management process for conversion in production of summary tables.

(*iii*) Being a part of query management process it facilitates to direct a query to the most appropriate data sources.

Due to variations in purpose its structure also varies in each process more details about metadata will be provided in later lecture notes.

(9) **End user Access tools:** To get appropriate information for strategic decision making, the business managers utilities data warehouse for this purpose. Thus to facilitate the user and warehouse interaction, the end user access tool is used.

(*i*) Reporting and Query Tools

(*ii*) Application Development Tools

(*iii*) Executive Information Systems Tools

(*iv*) Online Analytical Processing Tools

(*v*) Data Mining Tools

The E T L (Extract Transformation Load) Process

The four major process of the DATAWAREHOUSE are discussed in this section which as follows:

(*a*) **Extract:** Operational system data are brought to the DATAWAREHOUSE

(*b*) **Transform:** The data into internal formal & structures of the DATAWAREHOUSE according to the requirement.

(*c*) **Cleanse:** Quality of data is tested before it is used for decision making.

(*d*) **Load – Clauses data is put into the DATAWAREHOUSE:** The collection of all the four processer form extraction to loading is referred as data staging.

The four processes from extraction through loading often referred collectively as Data Staging.

Extract

The sorting of data from the operational database depending on the condition that which data elements can be expected to be useful in the decision making and which are less useful for that purpose can be necessarily extract before bringing it into the data warehouse. To support the extraction process many commercial equipments are available and data junction as one of the example.

Thus, to case the use of these equipments windows interface is provided to the user which specifies the following:

(*i*) Which files and tables are to be accessed in the source database?

(*ii*) Which fields are to be extracted from them? This is often done internally by SQL Select statement.

(*iii*) What are those to be called in the resulting database?

(*iv*) What is the target machine and database format of the output?

(*v*) On what schedule should the extraction process be repeated?

Transform

Any priority can be set before developing any operational data which might change according to the requirement. Therefore to avoid in consistency among their data sources, it can be rectified by adopting transformation process (if any).

One of the most common transformation issues is "Attribute Naming Inconsistency", and for data element it is commonly referred to by different names e.g., Employee name may be EMPNAME in one database, ENAME in the other. This set of Data Names are picked & used consistently in the data warehouse. Once all the data elements have right names, they must be converted to common formats. The conversion may encompass in the following way.

All these transformation activities are automated or converted and to support this many commercial products are available.

(*i*) Characters must be converted ASCII to EBCDIC or *vise versa.*

(*ii*) Mixed Text may be converted to all uppercase for consistency.

(*iii*) Numerical data must be converted into a common format.

(*iv*) Data Format has to be standardized.

(*v*) Measurement may have to convert. (***example*** $ to Rs.)

(*vi*) Coded data (Male/ Female, M/F) must be converted into a common format.

All these transformation activities are automated and many commercial products are available in the market. Data MAPPER is one such comprehensive tool given by Applied Database Technologies

Cleansing

The value of information is determined by the information quality. The quality of historic data cannot be changed randomly by any developer thus the data warehousing project always put their spotlight on the data quality issues and lead to provide improvements for the future. It is therefore, usually necessary to go through the data entered into the data warehouse and make it as error free as possible. This process is known as data cleansing.

Data cleansing handles many types of errors such as missing data, incorrect data at one source, inconsistent data & conflicting data etc.

Several algorithms are assigned to make the data error free which may be discussed.

Loading

Loading refers to physical movement of the data from staring the source database of the computer to that which will be stared into the data warehouse, assuming it is different. Just after the extraction phase, this movement takes place and the most common channel for data movement is a high speed communication link e.g., Oracle Warehouse builder is the API from Oracle which provides the features to perform the ETL task on ODW.

Data Mining

Data mining is the process of taking out potentially useful and unknown wide ranging information from large database which aims to focus on the most important information in their DATAWAREHOUSE. Data mining tools foretell upcoming trends and behaviors, allocating company to construct proactive, knowledge driven decisions.

The mechanized & computerized approach, which can construct the things automated, forthcoming analysis presented by data mining additionally ahead of the analyses of historical proceedings and events provided by retrospective tool representative of decision support systems. Data mining question can respond business questions that conventionally were time consuming. They search database for hidden outline, discovering extrapolative and predictive information to smoothen the progress of experts.

Most companies collect and get rid of massive data impurities. Data mining techniques can be put into practice rapidly on existing software and hardware platforms to enhance the value of existing information resources, and can be integrated with new products and systems as they are transported on line. When implemented on high performance client/server or parallel processing computers, data mining tools can analyze gigantic data to deliver answers to questions such as which clients are most likely to respond to the next promotional mailing and why?"

Data mining techniques have evolved from long processes of research and product development. This evolution began when data was traditionally stored in computers and kept on improving with the methods of data access till the time now when we can work with real time data. Data mining takes this evolutionary process beyond retrospective data access and navigation to prospective and proactive information delivery. Data mining is ready for application in the business community because it is supported by three technologies that are now sufficiently mature:

- Huge data collection
- Strong multiprocessor computers
- Data mining algorithms

Commercial databases are growing at unprecedented rates. A recent META Group survey of data warehouse projects found that 19% of respondents are beyond the 50 gigabyte level, while 59% expect to be there by second quarter of 1996. In some industries, mainly retail, these numbers are much bigger. With parallel multiprocessor computing technology need for improved computational engines can now be met in a cost-effective manner. Data mining algorithms symbolizes techniques that have existed for about a decade, but have only recently been implemented as mature, reliable, understandable tools that consistently outperform older statistical methods.

In the evolution from business data to business information, each new step has built upon the previous one. For example, dynamic data access is critical for drill-through in data navigation applications, and the ability to store large databases is critical to data mining. From the user's point of view, the four steps listed the given table which was revolutionary because they allowed new business questions to be answered accurately and quickly.

Evolutionary Step	Business Question	Enabling Technologies	Product Providers	Characteristics
Data Collection (1960s)	"What was the company's total revenue in the last five years?"	Computers, tapes, disks	IBM, CDC	Retrospective, static data delivery
Data Access (1980s)	"How many units were sold in Place X last March?"	Relational databases (RDBMS), Structured Query Language (SQL), ODBC	Oracle, Sybase, Informix, IBM, Microsoft	Retrospective, dynamic data delivery at record level
Data Warehousing & Decision Support (1990s)	"What were unit sales in Place last March?	On-line analytic processing (OLAP), multidimensional databases, data warehouses	Pilot, Comshare, Arbor, Cognos, Microstrategy	Retrospective, dynamic data delivery at multiple levels
Data Mining (Emerging Today)	"What's likely to happen to Place Y unit sales next month? Why?"	Advanced algorithms, multiprocessor computers, massive databases	Pilot, Lockheed, IBM, SGI, numerous startups (nascent industry)	Prospective, proactive information delivery

Table Steps in the Evolution of Data Mining

From decades, there have been developments in the core components of data mining technology i.e. in research areas such as statistics, Artificial Intelligence and machine learning. Today, these techniques are the base of life, coupled with high performance relational database engines and data integration efforts, which make their technologies practical for currant data warehouse environments.

The Scope of Data Mining

The term data mining has originated from the similitude between searching for essential business information in a large database and mining a mountain for a crack in rock for valuable ore. Both of these processes require either movement through a huge amount of material or intelligently investigating exactly where the value resides. Given database of sufficient size and quality, data mining technology can generate new business opportunities by providing these capabilities.

Data mining mechanizes the procedure of finding predictive information in large databases. Due to data availability traditional question required extensive hands-on-analysis can be answered rapidly. Targeted problem is the ultimate example of predictive problem.

Future mailing rotenone investment can be maximized, as data mining uses data on past promotional mailings to identify the targets. Forecasting bankruptcy, others forms of default & identifying segments of a population likely to respond similarly to givens events are few more predictive problems.

Data mining tools traverses through database and identify patterns in one step. An example of pattern recognition is the examination of retail sales data to identify seemingly unrelated products that are often purchased together. Detesting fraudulent credit card transactions & identifying anomalous data that could represent data entry explanation errors are few more patterns discover problems.

The benefits of automation capitulate on currently available software & hardware platforms and can be implemented on new systems as current platforms are promoted and new products are developed by data mining techniques. Due to implementation of data mining tools on high performance parallel processing systems they can analyze huge database in minutes.

Rapid processing means that users can automatically conduct experiment with more models to appropriate complex data and due to high speed, huge quantities of data can be easily analyzed by users. Larger databases in turn yield improved forecast.

Analysts should limit the number of variables when they do hands on analysis due to time constraints. Yet variables are redundant because they give the impressions as unimportant that may carry information about unknown patterns. User can explore full depth of a database, without pre selecting a subset of variables as a result of high perfọrmance data mining.

Users are permitted to make inferences about small but important segments of a population because larger samples yield lower estimation errors and variance.

Techniques used in data mining are:

1. Artificial neural networks: Non linear predictive models that will learn through training and be similar to biological neural networks in structure.

2. Decision trees: Tree shaped structures that keep up a correspondence to sets of decisions and rules for the classification of a data set is also engender by these decisions. CART (Classification and Regression Trees) and CHAID (Chi Square Automatic Interaction Detection) are specific decision tree .

3. Genetic algorithms: Optimization techniques that bring into play processes such as genetic combination, mutation and normal selection in a design, based on the concepts of evolution.

4. Nearest neighbor: In pattern recognition, the ***k*-nearest neighbor algorithm** (*k*-NN) is a method for classifying objects by a majority vote of its neighbors, with the object being assigned to the class most common amongst its *k* nearest neighbors (*k* is a positive integer, typically small). If $k = 1$, then the object is simply assigned to the class of its nearest neighbor.

5. Rule induction: data based on statistical significance, the extraction of useful if-then rules.

6. Data visualization: The visual interpretation of complex relationships in multidimensional data. Graphics tools are used to illustrate data relationships.

Use of these technologies in specialized examination tools for more than a decide that works with modularity small volumes of data. These capabilities are now surfacing to integrate directly with industry standard data warehouse and OLAP platforms.

Data Mining Mechanism

Data mining is a logical process that is used to search through large amounts of information in order to find important data. The goal of this technique is to find patterns that were previously unknown. Once that has done, it can be used to solve a number of problems.

Stage 1: Exploration: As the name implies it helps to explore and prepare the data. It may be needed that the data is cleaned or transformed to another form. In addition to this there can be a need to create records. If there are larger numbers of variables it may need to be reduced to a range which is easily manageable.

Based on the problem that is to be solved, need may arise to either come up with a number of predictions, or to use a wider selection of tools in order to analyze the data. An example of tools used are graphs and statistics. The goal of the exploration stage is to find important variables and determine their nature.

Stage 2: Pattern Identification. In this step it is required to look for patterns and choose one that will help to make the best predictions. This stage of data mining is a bit complex. There are a wide variety of different ways which can find the best predictive patterns. One of the best ways to do this is to apply different patterns to a given situation to determine which one performs at the highest level. For example, if the need is to look at data to find patterns that will help a store to earn more profits, two shopping patterns of customers can be traced and apply them to a hypothetical strategy to determine which one performs the best.

Stage 3: Deployment: Until a consistent pattern is obtained from stage 2 that is highly predictive, it is not advisable to move to this step.

For example, if it is found that many customers are consistently buying a specific product on a certain date, their future behavior can be predicted. This pattern can be applied on the data in order to see if desired outcome can be achieved. Data mining has become a popular term among many companies and organizations.

For example: Data mining in customer relationship management applications can contribute significantly. Rather than randomly contacting a prospect or customer through a call center or sending mail, a company can concentrate its efforts on prospects that are predicted to have a high likelihood of responding to an offer. More sophisticated methods may be used to optimize resources across campaigns so that one may predict to which channel and to which offer an individual is most likely to respond—across all potential offers. Additionally, sophisticated applications could be used to automate the mailing. Once the results from data mining (potential prospect/customer and channel/offer) are determined, this "sophisticated application" can either automatically send an e-mail or regular mail. Finally, in cases where many people will take an action without an offer, uplift modeling can be used to determine which people will have the greatest increase in responding if given an offer

[*source: Wikipedia*]

Architecture for Data Mining

These can be utilized if it is properly integrated with DATAWAREHOUSE and interactive business analysis tools. Data mining tools most perform their operations outside the warehouse, requiring extra steps for extracting, importing, and analyzing the data but when new insights require operational implementation, integration with the warehouse simplifies the application of results from data mining. The outcome of these analytic data can be used in areas such as promotional campaign management, fraud detection, new product rollout etc.

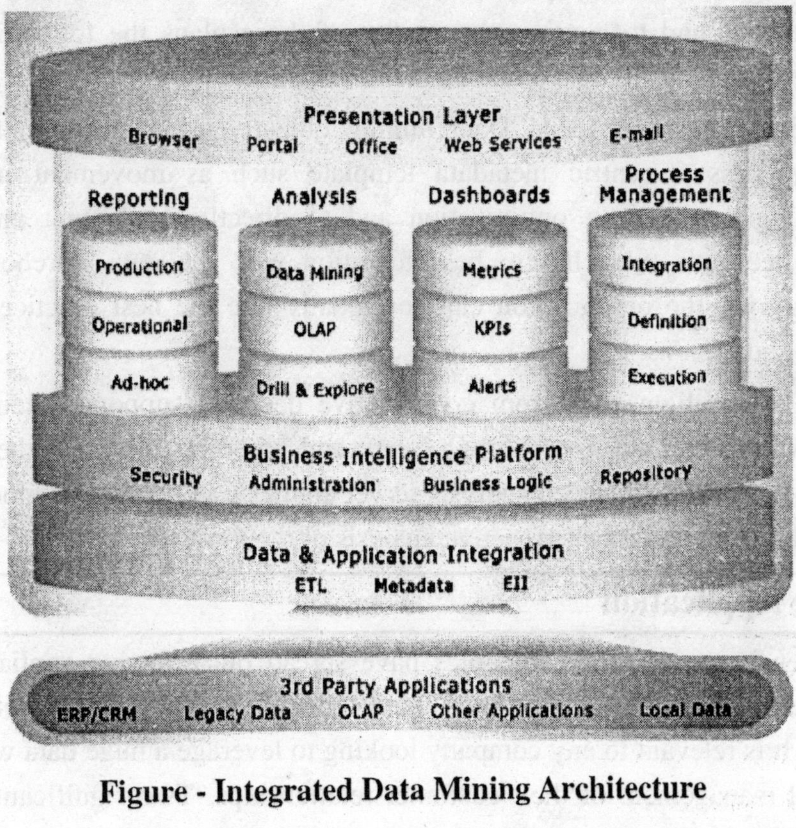

Figure - Integrated Data Mining Architecture

The perfect starting point is a DATAWAREHOUSE which is a combination of internal data pathway of all contact customers, coupled with outside market data about competitor activity. The details of background information on potential customer also provide an excellent basis for prospecting. This warehouse can be put into practice in a multiplicity of relational database systems. Sybase, Oracle, Redbrick, etc. and should be achieved for flexible and fast data access.

To ease the navigation across the DATAWAREHOUSE an OIAP server is applied which provides a more sophisticated end user business model. Its multidimensional structures permit the user to analyze the data, as they want to view their business summarizing by product line, region, and other key perspectives of their business. The data mining server included as a part with the data warehouse and the OLAP forever to directing fixe or erupted ROI focused business analysis directly into this infrastructure.

OLAP server can be modified as its results enhances the metadata by providing a dynamic metadata layer that represents a distilled view of the data as well as to sketch the future actions and to confirm the impact of those plans the following reporting visualization & other analytical total can then be applied.

For specific business usual Data mining objectives have been defined by an advanced, process – centric metadata template such as movement management, prospecting, and promotion optimization and to directly implement and track the operational decisions there has to be integration with the data warehouse. As the warehouse grows, the organization can continually line the best practices and apply them to future decisions.

This is a paradigm shift from conservative decision support system to simply delivering data to the end user through query and reporting software, there has been elementary shift as the advanced analysis server applies user's business models directly to the warehouse and returns a proactive analysis of the most relevant.

Profitable Application

An extensive variety of companies have spread out effective appliance of data mining. Financial services and direct mail marketing are early adopters of this technology. It is relevant to any company looking to leverage a huge data warehouse to an enhanced management of their customer relationships. Two significant factors for success with data mining are:

Some successful application areas include:

1. Retail stores routinely use data mining tools to learn about purchasing habits of its customers. Eg. Amazon.com uses data mining to provide customers with purchase suggestions: Customers who bought this book also bought: Seven Methods for Transforming Corporate Data Into Business Intelligence by Vasant Dhar, Roger Stein Building Data Mining Applications for CRM by Alex Berson, et al Data Preparation for Data Mining by Dorian Pyle Kellogg on Integrated Marketing by Dawn Iacobucci (Editor), et al Multivariate Data Analysis (5th Edition) by Joseph F. Hair (Editor), et al Explore similar items.
2. A credit card company can leverage its vast warehouse of customer transaction data to identify customers most likely to be interested in a new credit product. Using a small test mailing, the attributes of customers with an affinity for the product can be identified. Recent projects have indicated more than a 20-fold decrease in costs for targeted mailing campaigns over conventional approaches.
3. A diversified transportation company with a large direct sales force can apply data mining to identify the best prospects for its services. Using data mining to analyze its own customer experience, this company can build a unique segmentation identifying the attributes of high-value prospects. Applying this segmentation to a general business database such as those provided by Dun & Bradstreet can yield a prioritized list of prospects by region.

Data mining parameters

- ***Association*** - looking for patterns where one event is connected to another event
- ***Sequence or path analysis*** - looking for patterns where one event leads to another later event
- ***Classification*** - looking for new patterns (May result in a change in the way the data is organized but that's ok)
- ***Clustering*** - finding and visually documenting groups of facts not previously known

- *Forecasting* - discovering patterns in data that can lead to reasonable predictions about the future (This area of data mining is known as predictive analytics).

Data mining is useful in investigation and research area such as Mathematics, Cybernetics, and Genetics & Marketing.

Data Mining Include

1. Knowledge Discovery: The objective of knowledge discovery is to identify meaningful data patterns, hidden relationships or correlations in an Enterprise's database, Data mining can be used to performs.

(1) Segmentation

(2) Classification

(3) Association

(4) Referencing

2. Visualize data: Visualizing data is the main target of data mining

3. Correct data: identifying problems and correcting them can be easily handled by data mining technique in a very consistent way.

On line Analytical Processing (OLAP)

OLAP software can evaluate real time analysis of data stored in a database. The OLAP source is an independent tool that contains specialized algorithm and indexing features to efficiently process data mining with negligible impact on database performance.

Sorting, extracting & viewing of data can be easily done by user through OLAP.

Example: companies have many dimensions to track-like, a business that distributes goods from more than a single facility will have at least the following Dimensions to consider: Accounts, Locations, Periods, Salespeople and Products. These Dimensions comprise a base for the company's planning, analysis and reporting activities. Together they represent the whole business picture, providing the foundation for all business planning, analysis and reporting activities

For the discovery of undisclosed relationship between data items and data mining activities, OLAP can be utilized. Size of OLAP database is comparatively smaller that data warehouse since all transaction data is not needed for trend analysis. To transfer the data from existing relational database to create a multidimensional database, an ODBC (Open Database Connectivity) can be used.

OLAP products support multiuser environment depending on the cost of the software based on the number of users. Two popular OLAP products are Hyperion solution's & Oracle's Express Server.

OLAP is application architecture, not a data warehouse or a DBMS(data base management System). Thus to support analytical applications increasing number of enterprises are implementing an OLAP architecture. Dr. E. Do Dweld, the father of relational model, has formulated a list of 12 guidelines

(1) Multidimensional conceptual view
(2) Transparency
(3) Accessibility
(4) Consistent reporting performance
(5) Client/server architecture
(6) Generic dimensionality
(7) Dynamic sparse matrix handling
(8) Multiuser support
(9) Unrestricted cross dimensional operations
(10) Intuitive data manipulation
(11) Flexible reporting
(12) Unlimited dimensions & aggregative levels

OLAP is based on multidimensional database technology and provides multi-dimensional views of business data that provides the technical basis for calculations & analysis required by business intelligence application. It also describes a class of technologies that are designed for live data access & analysis while transaction processing (OLAP) generally relies on relational database.

OLAP technology supports and is used in an variety of applications such as for sales and making analysis, financial reporting & budgeting & planning, for product projectability and pricing analysis, activity based on costing, men power planning &

quality analysis, or for that matter any management system that requires a flexible top down view of an organization

Product Life Cycle Management

PLM is a process that puts in a consistent set of business solution in support of the information required for mutual creation, management, dissemination, use of product and concept to end of life of product by integrating people, processes, business systems, and information across the enterprise involving strategic business

Product life cycle management is one of the most necessary part of enterprise information technology structure. All companies are required to organize communication and information with customer (Customer Relationship Management), theirs supplier (Supply Chain Management), their resources within the enterprise (ERP) and planning the process (system development life cycle-SDLC). To top up this manufacturing and engineering companies need to develop, describes, organizes and communicate information about the product.

People centric PLM is the form of PLM which is targeted at the design phase and traditional PLM is targeted during the release phase

Recent development in information and communication technology, has permitted PLM to stretch-out further beyond traditional PLM and integrates real time life cycle event and data into it. It is also allowed in the total life cycle of an individual product that information is provided to different player. As a result PLM gets extended into closed loop life cycle management (CL_2M).

Introduction to Product Life Cycle Management

Data related to the designing, production support and ultimate disposal of manufactured good's is managed by PLM. PLM has emerged from CAD (Computer Aided Designing) CAM(Computer Aided Manufacturing) and PDM(Product Data Management), but it can be conceived as integration of people and processes through all stages of a product's life Since a decade manufacturers, industrial machinery, packed goods and other complex engineered product have found out the advantage of PLM solutions and due to this PLM software are adopted in large number.

PLM Solutions

(*a*) PLM is a repository of all data that affects a product.

(*b*) PLM can be considered as a commercial process between stockholder, marketing, engineering, manufacturing and field service.

Information from marketing and designing comes together only in one place which is PLM system where it comes in the form which is appropriate for production and support.

Some analysts use world P^2M (Product Portfolio Management) which includes engineering CAD. PLM concentrate mainly on data management that covers the breadth of product life cycle.

Crucial elements of PLM are.

- Manages **design and process documents**
- Constructs and controls **bill of material** (product structure) records
- Offers an **electronic file repository**
- Includes built-in and custom **part and document metadata** ("attributes")
- Identifies **materials content for environmental compliance**
- Permits **item-focused task assignments**
- Enables **workflow and process management** for approving changes
- Controls **multi-user secured access**, including "electronic signature"
- Exports **data for downstream ERP systems**

Advantages

Product lifecycle management include following document benefits:

(1) Reduce time to market

(2) Product quality gets better

(3) Reduce prototyping cost

(4) Exactly and Timely request for quote generation.

(5) Power to fact recognize the potential sales opportunity and sales contribution

(6) Cost saving through reuse of original data.

(7) A framework for product optimization

(8) Reduces waste

(9) Saving through complete integration of work frame

(10) Ability to provide contracts manufacturers with access to a centralized product record.

Areas of PLM

There are five primary owners inside PLM

1. Systems Engineering (SE) : SE focuses on dealing with complex engineering projects, on how to design and manage the life cycle of the project. It deals with work-processes and tools to handle these projects, and overlaps with both technical and human-centered disciplines such as control engineering, industrial engineering, organizational studies, and project management
2. Product and Portfolio Management (PPM) : PPM describes methods for analyzing current or proposed projects based on numerous key characteristics. The fundamental objective of PPM is to determine the best possible mix and sequencing of proposed projects to best achieve the organization's overall goals
3. Product Design (CAD) : Product design focuses on efficient and effective generation and development of ideas through a process that leads to new products
4. Manufacturing Process Management (MPM) : MPM deals with the planning or forecasting or marketing of one or more products in all stages of the product lifecycle.
5. Product Data Management (PDM): PDM is a sub process in PLM which is responsible for the creation, management and publication of product data

Development Process

The centre part of PLM is in the making and central organizing of all data product and the technology used to execute information & knowledge PLM comes from the CAD/CAM & PDM, and can be seen as the integration of these tools with methods, people & the processes through all stages of product life. It is about software as well as business strategy. There is a variation in elder of event & tasks with respect to product & industry in question but main process as are:

1. Conceive

- Specification
- Concept design

2. Design

- Detailed design
- Validation & analysis
- Total design

3. Realize

- Plan Manufacturing
- Manufacture
- Build/Assemble
- Test (Quality Check)

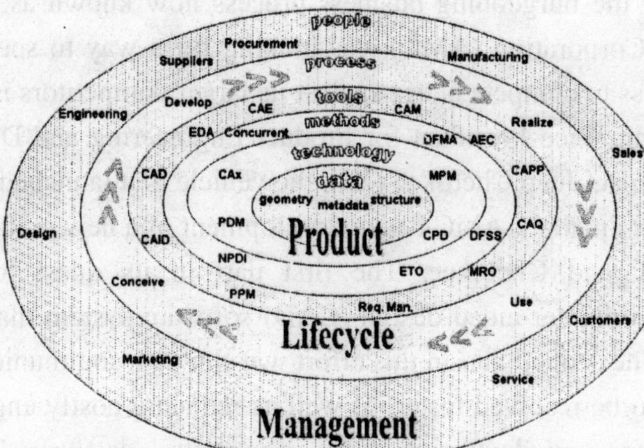

Figure: PLM Development Process

Source: Wikipedia

4. Service

- Sell and Deliver
- Use
- Maintain and Support
- Dispose

The important key point events are

- Order

- Idea
- Kick Off
- Design Freeze
- Launch.

There is more complexities in reality. People and department are not able to carry out their tasks in solution and without the completion of previous activity the next activity get started design is a repetitive process which required some partial changes due to manufacturing constraints or conflicting requirement. In time live it depends on industry type when exactly customer order fits.

History

Inspiration for the burgeoning business process now known as PLM came when American Motors Corporation (AMC) was looking for a way to speed up its product development process to compete better against its larger competitors in 1985, according to François Castaing, Vice President for Product Engineering and Development After introducing its compact Jeep Cherokee (XJ), the vehicle that launched the modern sport utility vehicle (SUV) market, AMC began development of a new model, that later came out as the Jeep Grand Cherokee. The first part in its quest for faster product development was computer-aided design (CAD) software system that make engineers more productive. The second part in this effort was the new communication system that allowed conflicts to be resolved faster, as well as reducing costly engineering changes because all drawings and documents were in a central database. The product data management was so effective, that after AMC was purchased by Chrysler, the system was expanded throughout the enterprise connecting everyone involved in designing and building products. While an early adopter of PLM technology, Chrysler was able to become the auto industry's lowest-cost producer, recording development costs that were half of the industry average by the mid-1990s

Phases of product lifecycle and corresponding technologies

To arrange and integrate the different phases of product lifecycle today many software solutions have been developed. PLM is seen as a collection of software tools & working method that combines together to address single stage of lifecycle or join different task to organize the whole process.

The basic goal of PLM is to accumulate knowledge that can be used again for other project and work effectively together for development of many products, PLM is basically corrected with engineering work & it also includes marketing activities such as product portfolio, specially with regards to New Product Introduction (NPI).

Phase 1: Conceive (Imagine, specify, plan, and innovate)

The initial stage involves the definition of its needs passed on to customers, company, market and regulatory bodies. Form this detailed description of product or usually technical parameter can be explained, precisely similar requirements and specification describes scope of the usual authenticity of product along with its important functions and aspects which is carried out by the initial concept design work. The tools required for designing of styling industrial work include media like pencil & paper, clay models to 3 D CAID (Computer Aided Industrial Design Software System).

Phase 2: Design (Describe, define, develop, test, analyze and validate)

In this phase beginning of detailed design and growing of product starts, improving prototype testing, launch of full product through pilot allow to more. Form making improvement is the existing product along with planned obsolescence. It should also include redesign and platform for improvement to existing products. CAD is the basic equipment utilized in development and it can also be simplified 2D drawing draft or 3D parametric feature based solid / surface modeling. And the technology is included in such software are HM(Hybrid Modeling), RE(Reverse Engineering,), KBE (Knowledge-Based Engineering), NDT(Nondestructive testing), AC(Assembly construction).

Many engineering disciplines are covered by these step which involve mechanical, electrical electronic, software and domain specific like architecture aerospace, Automotive, beside the geometry creation there is also the detailed examination of the component & product assemblies. CAE (Computer-aided engineering) software can be utilized for the task like simulation, validation and optimization which is either integrated in the CAD package or stand along. These are used to perform following tasks. Like stress analysis FEA (Finite Element Analysis), Kinematic, computational fluid dynamics and mechanical event stimulation (MES), CAQ (Computer-aided quality) is used for tasks such as Dimensional Tolerance Analysis.

Phase 3: Realize (Manufacture, make, build, procure, produce, sell and deliver)

This method of manufacturing defines only when the design of products and component is complete. This may involve CAD task such as tool design for the product's part, CNC matching, have been developed and tools for manufacturing those parts by using integrated or separate CAM software. This also includes tool analysis for the action such as casting, molding and die press forming. As the method of manufacturing is discovered CPM comes into action. This involves CAPE(Computer-aided Production Engineering) or CAP/CAPP(Computer-aided Production Planning) tools to be used in factory plant and facility layout & production stimulation. For instance Press-Line Stimulation and Industrial Ergonomics as well as tool selection management. By using computer aided inspection equipment and software given ethical form & size can be examine in opposition to the original Computer Aided data.

Parallel to the engineering tasks, sales product configuration and much documentation work will be taking place. This may involve transferring engineering data to a web based sale configuration and other desktop publishing system.

Phase 4: Service (Use, operate, maintain, support, sustain, phase-out, retire, recycle and disposal)

At the end phase of life cycle includes organizing of service information. customers and service engineers are provided with support information and these information are like repair & maintenance as well as waste management / recycling information. Tools like maintenance repair and operation management software are involve in this.

Supply Chain Management (SCM)

Supply chain management is the process by which planning and management of all activities involved in sourcing, procurement, conversion, and logistics management is done . It includes the vital elements of coordination and collaboration with suppliers, intermediaries, third-party service providers, and customers. Real meaning of supply chain management is integrating supply and demand within and across companies

Supply Chain Decisions

The various decisions taken in SCM are in three levels. Namely, Operational level, Tactical level and Strategic level. Activities at each level can be summarized as:-

Operational level

The key areas in this level are:-

1. Day to day production and distribution planning,

2. Production scheduling for each manufacturing facility
3. Demand planning and forecasting,.
4. Sourcing planning, including current inventory and demand forecast, in collaboration with the suppliers.
5. Inbound operations, including transportation from suppliers and receiving inventory.
6. Production operations like consumption of materials and flow of finished goods.
7. Outbound operations like warehousing and transportation to customers.
8. Order promising to all suppliers, manufacturing facilities, distribution centers, and other customers.
9. From production level to supply level accounting all transit damage cases & arrange to settlement at customer level by maintaining company loss through insurance company.

Tactical level

1. Sourcing contracts and purchasing decisions.
2. Production decisions as in contracting, scheduling, and planning process definition.
3. Inventory decisions which includes quantity, location, and quality of inventory.
4. Transportation strategy, including frequency, routes, and contracting.
5. Standardizing of all operations against competitors and implementation of best practices throughout the enterprise.

Strategic level

1. Strategic network optimization like deciding the number, location, and size of warehousing, distribution centers, and facilities.
2. Long term partnerships with suppliers, distributors, and customers, so as to create a communication channel for information and operational improvements such as cross docking, direct shipping, and third-party logistics.

3. Product life cycle management, so that new and existing products can be optimally integrated into the supply chain and capacity management activities.
4. Information technology chain operations.
5. Where-to-make and make-buy decisions.
6. Streamlining overall organizational strategy with supply strategy.
7. Keep a constant vigil on customer demand and behavior

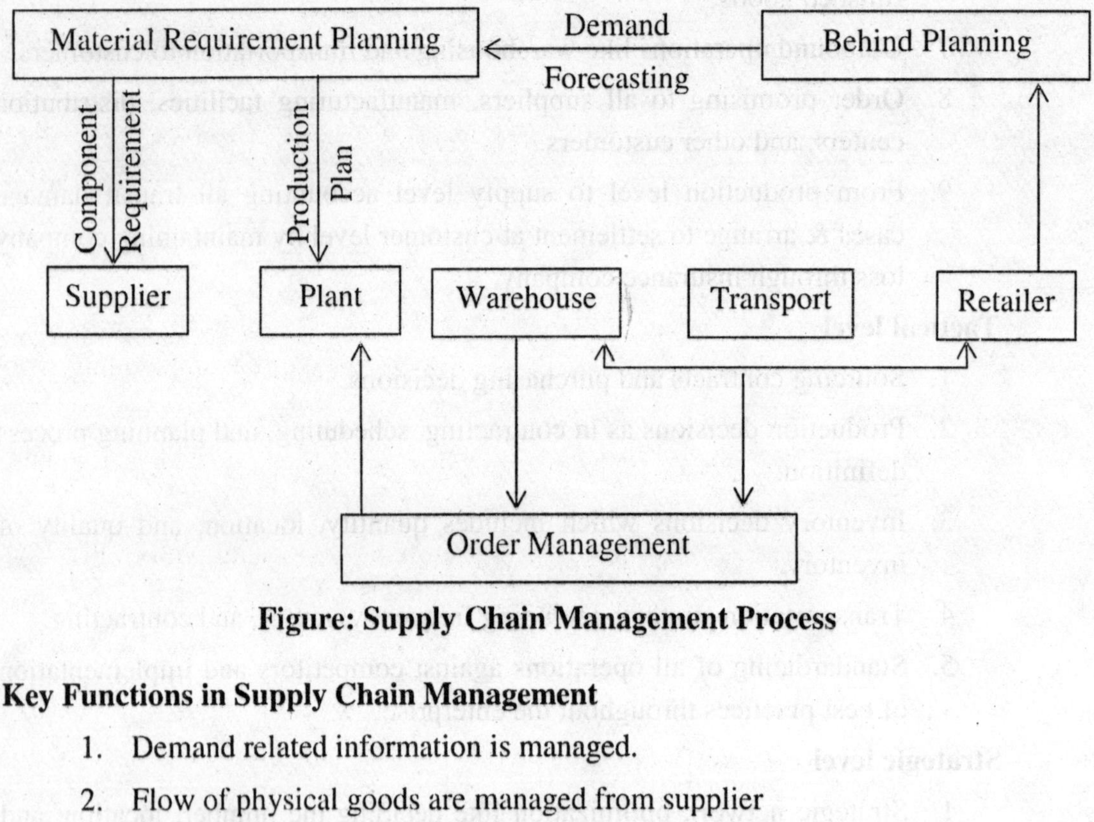

Figure: Supply Chain Management Process

Key Functions in Supply Chain Management

1. Demand related information is managed.
2. Flow of physical goods are managed from supplier
3. With supplier and customer financial flow get manages.
4. Reduction in lead time
5. Reduces the number of stages
6. Improved flexibility
7. Improved process quality
8. Demand get managed

Some of the software used in SCM are:

- **People soft**
- **Ariba** spend management
- **SAP**
- **BAAN**
- **LSE: SGE** from The Sage Group plc, commonly known as **Sage,**
- **IES, Ltd.:** Supply chain management software company that develops software for freight forwarders, Customs brokers
- **Oracle**

Benefit of SCM

- Reduction in inventory level
- Reduces mark down and scrap
- Efficient use of resources
- Reducing transportation cost

SCM is connected with the supplier, manufacturing, assembly, distribution & logistic facilities that goes through the function of procurement of material, manufacturing finished product & then sending of these product to customer. Supply Chain originated in both manufacturing and service organization.

SCM manages whole flow of information, material and service from raw material supplier through factories and warehouses to end customer. SCM is unlike :om supply management which stresses on buyer supplier relationship only

Element of SCM

There are six key elements to a supply chain:

1. **Production:** Production focus on what customers want and the market demands
2. **Supply:** this focuses on carefully selecting suppliers for raw materials. The vital facts that should be kept in mind while choosing a supplier are less time and reducing costs
3. **Inventory:** focus on inventory and how much product should be in-house. Control policies must be looked at to determine correct levels of supplies at order and reorder points.

4. **Location**: Location decisions depend on market demands and determination of customer satisfaction. Once customer markets are determined, long-term commitment must be made to locate production and stocking facilities
5. **Transportation**: Since using the correct transport mode is a critical strategic decision thus an organization should posses proper transportation facility to ensure a smooth distribution of goods.
6. **Information**: For ensuring speedy exchange of information in the entire supply chain connecting computers by networks like intranet, internet, is required. This will ensure streamlining the information flow in the entire chain.

Scope of SCM

The range and scope of SCM can be identified as :

1. **Supplier Management:** Material that is procured from different supplier is the most critical resources for manufacturing firm. For easy and smooth production it is very important to have smooth flow of material. Supplier management takes care of this process.
2. **Inventory Management:** SCM mainly is concerned with maximizing performance in a reduced inventory level. Stocking policies and inventory level is assumed by inventory decision. Stock policies find out precisely where inventory is stored or maintained and its reorder level. It is also concerned with cost of carrying inventory and risk of stocking
3. **Distribution Management:** This is related to transportation of finished product to the end users. Transportation costs involve distance volume, density, stability, handling, liability and market factors. In many logistics operation transportation is involves a huge cost.
4. **Channel Management:** Channels are seen as a system of connectors or association among businesses that involves in the process of purchasing and selling products & services. The aim of SCM is to grow a successful channel arrangement with the help of economics of distribution channel. The total characteristic of channel structure needs to complete the marketing process which involves wholesalers and retailers. The whole supply chain is planned in a way so that right products are present at the right place at right time.

5. **Payment Management:** Payment management at correct time intensify or improves the relationships among the members in the chain and keep up their goodwill.
6. **Financial Management:** For strategic decision data from SCM can be utilized by chief financial officers in for funding in the entire process.
7. **Sales Force Management:** SCM gives complete satisfaction to the customer by supporting the sales staff. Easy follow up is provided by information., checking credit online, on proposal submitted by the sales force providing dealer contacts to promote use of advertising packages.

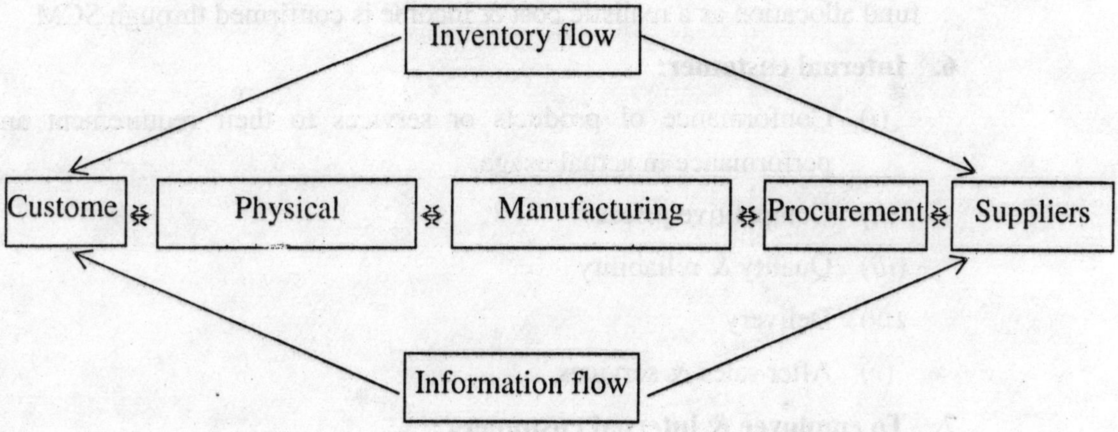

Advantage of SCM

1. **To Supplier:**
   - (*i*) By using internet or e-mail, information and instruction related to goods can be easily disseminated
   - (*ii*) It reduces paper work by transferring data online.
2. **Inventory Economy:**
   - (*i*) Low cost of holding inventory, as the optimum inventory management parameters that meet desired service levels with minimum investment is determined.
   - (*ii*) Low risk of stock by deciding on the optimum size of replenishment orders and the necessary reorder points.

3. **Distribution Efficiency:**

   (*i*) Satisfied distributors and whole sales ensure that the right products reach the right place at right time.

   (*ii*) Easy accounting of stock and cost of stock.

4. **Channel Management:**

   To provide product assortment a channel structure significantly reduces the total cost of transaction required.

5. **Financial Management:**

   Funds are used for crucial assignments. There is a possibility of priotizing of fund allocation as a realistic cost & income is confirmed through SCM.

6. **Internal customer:**

   (*i*) Conformance of products or services to their requirement and its performance in actual usage.

   (*ii*) Competitive prices

   (*iii*) Quality & reliability

   (*iv*) Delivery

   (*v*) After sales & services.

7. **To employee & internal customers :**

   (*i*) Teamwork & co-operation

   (*ii*) Efficient structure & systems

   (*iii*) Quality work

   (*iv*) Delivery

Glossary of Data Mining Terms

analytical model	A structure and process for analyzing a dataset. For example, a decision tree is a model for the classification of a dataset.
anomalous data	Data that result from errors (for example, data entry keying errors) or that represent unusual events. Anomalous data should be examined carefully because it may carry important information.

artificial neural networks	Non-linear predictive models that learn through training and resemble biological neural networks in structure.
CART	Classification and Regression Trees. A decision tree technique used for classification of a dataset. Provides a set of rules that you can apply to a new (unclassified) dataset to predict which records will have a given outcome. Segments a dataset by creating 2-way splits. Requires less data preparation than CHAID.
CHAID	Chi Square Automatic Interaction Detection. A decision tree technique used for classification of a dataset. Provides a set of rules that you can apply to a new (unclassified) dataset to predict which records will have a given outcome. Segments a dataset by using chi square tests to create multi-way splits. Preceded, and requires more data preparation than, CART.
classification	The process of dividing a dataset into mutually exclusive groups such that the members of each group are as "close" as possible to one another, and different groups are as "far" as possible from one another, where distance is measured with respect to specific variable(s) you are trying to predict. For example, a typical classification problem is to divide a database of companies into groups that are as homogeneous as possible with respect to a creditworthiness variable with values "Good" and "Bad."
clustering	The process of dividing a dataset into mutually exclusive groups such that the members of each group are as "close" as possible to one another, and different groups are as "far" as possible from one another, where distance is measured with respect to all available variables.
data cleansing	The process of ensuring that all values in a dataset are consistent and correctly recorded.
data mining	The extraction of hidden predictive information from large databases.

data navigation	The process of viewing different dimensions, slices, and levels of detail of a multidimensional database. See OLAP.
data visualization	The visual interpretation of complex relationships in multidimensional data.
data warehouse	A system for storing and delivering massive quantities of data.
decision tree	A tree-shaped structure that represents a set of decisions. These decisions generate rules for the classification of a dataset. See CART and CHAID.
dimension	In a flat or relational database, each field in a record represents a dimension. In a multidimensional database, a dimension is a set of similar entities; for example, a multidimensional sales database might include the dimensions Product, Time, and City.
exploratory data analysis	The use of graphical and descriptive statistical techniques to learn about the structure of a dataset.
genetic algorithms	Optimization techniques that use processes such as genetic combination, mutation, and natural selection in a design based on the concepts of natural evolution.
linear model	An analytical model that assumes linear relationships in the coefficients of the variables being studied.
linear regression	A statistical technique used to find the best-fitting linear relationship between a target (dependent) variable and its predictors (independent variables).
logistic regression	A linear regression that predicts the proportions of a categorical target variable, such as type of customer, in a population.
multidimensional database	A database designed for on-line analytical processing. Structured as a multidimensional hypercube with one axis per dimension.
multiprocessor computer	A computer that includes multiple processors connected by a network. See parallel processing.

nearest neighbor	A technique that classifies each record in a dataset based on a combination of the classes of the k record(s) most similar to it in a historical dataset (where k ³ 1). Sometimes called a k-nearest neighbor technique.
non-linear model	An analytical model that does not assume linear relationships in the coefficients of the variables being studied.
OLAP	On-line analytical processing. Refers to array-oriented database applications that allow users to view, navigate through, manipulate, and analyze multidimensional databases.
outlier	A data item whose value falls outside the bounds enclosing most of the other corresponding values in the sample. May indicate anomalous data. Should be examined carefully; may carry important information.
parallel processing	The coordinated use of multiple processors to perform computational tasks. Parallel processing can occur on a multiprocessor computer or on a network of workstations or PCs.
predictive model	A structure and process for predicting the values of specified variables in a dataset.
prospective data analysis	Data analysis that predicts future trends, behaviors, or events based on historical data.
RAID	Redundant Array of Inexpensive Disks. A technology for the efficient parallel storage of data for high-performance computer systems.
retrospective data analysis	Data analysis that provides insights into trends, behaviors, or events that have already occurred.
rule induction	The extraction of useful if-then rules from data based on statistical significance.
SMP	Symmetric multiprocessor. A type of multiprocessor computer

	in which memory is shared among the processors.
terabyte	One trillion bytes.
time series analysis	The analysis of a sequence of measurements made at specified time intervals. Time is usually the dominating dimension of the data.

REVIEW QUESTIONS

1. What is ERP?
2. What are the limitations of ERP?
3. What is BPR?
4. What is MIS?
5. What is DSS and how is it different from MIS?
6. What is EIS?
7. What is data warehousing?
8. What is data mining?
9. What do you mean by OLAP?
10. Explain the concept of supply chain management?
11. Define Business Process Reengineering? Illustrate it with a suitable example?
12. Distinguish BPR and ERP?
13. Discuss the process involved in BPR? Explain it with the help of diagram?
14. What are the Re-engineering proposal?
15. What are the characteristics elements and nature of SCM.
16. Write the concept of SCM?
17. What are the benefits of supply chain management?
18. Distinguish between ERP and SCM?
19. What are the components of SCM?
20. Why SCM is necessary for any organization? Given any example.

21. Define model of SCM.
22. How does supply chain Management Evolves?
23. What should be implement in SCM?
24. Define Data mining? Explain it with the help of case analysis.
25. What are the steps involved in the evolution of data mining?
26. What is the scope of data mining?
27. How data mining can be mechanised?
28. What are the areas of application of data mining?
29. What are the various methods used in Data mining?
30. What are the approaches used in data mining?
31. What is data warehouse & decision support.
32. What do you're mean by data warehouse?
33. Define data mart? Explain it with the help of diagram?
34. What are the fetuses of data warehouse?
35. Explain OLAP model?
36. What do we need data warehouse?
37. What are the basic components required for data warehouse?
38. Explain the different layers of data warehouse?
39. How we can manage data warehouse?
40. What are the different stages of date warehouse?
41. What are the failure & benefits of data warehousing. Explain in detail?
42. "Data warehouse is subject oriented integrated time variant and non-volatile collection of Data". Explain this statement?
43. Define the data warehouse in Indian Context?
44. Write Tendencies of data warehouse.
45. Explain Product life cycle management (PLM)?

3 ERP Marketplace and Marketplace Dynamics

Market Overview

As stated by AMR Research (now part of Gartner, the leading provider of research and analysis on the global IT industry.), the ERP market is very competitive and significantly growing.

Three primary factures of AMR research that attributes the continued growth in ERP market:

- ERP vendors are seeking to expand market by contributing new application such as supply chain management, sales force automation, customer support and human resource.
- ERP vendors focus to accelerate the sales of licenses into their installed systems so as to sustain their rapid growth. At present 10-20% penetrations are provided to ERP vendors.
- Due to origin of ERP in the manufacturing market, ERP usage has expanded to almost every type of enterprise including retail, The public sector and health care organization. Thus the trend to purchase new ERP system for the first time also increased over the next 5 years.

The vendors in the ERP market focuses on expanded product functionality, new target markets and higher penetration rates. They are segregated in two segments. The top tier segment consists of 5 vendors SAP AG, Baan, People soft, Oracle applications & JD Edwards. These 5 big companies account for 64% of the ERP market revenue and over the past year the growth rate has shown tremendous increase of 61%. The table under (Compiled from Panorama Consulting data)

Sample Vendors		
Tier I	**Tier II**	**Tier III**
SAP	Epicor	ABAS
Oracle	Sage	Activant Solutions Inc.
Oracle eBusiness Suite	Infor	Bowen and Groves
Oracle JD Edwards	IFS	Compiere
Oracle Peoplesoft	QAD	Exact
Misrosoft Dynamics	Lawson	NetSuite
	CDC Software	Visibility
		CGS
		Hansa World
		Consona
		Syspro

Shown below is the ERP market share at 2009 between Tier II and top 3 Tier I vendors.

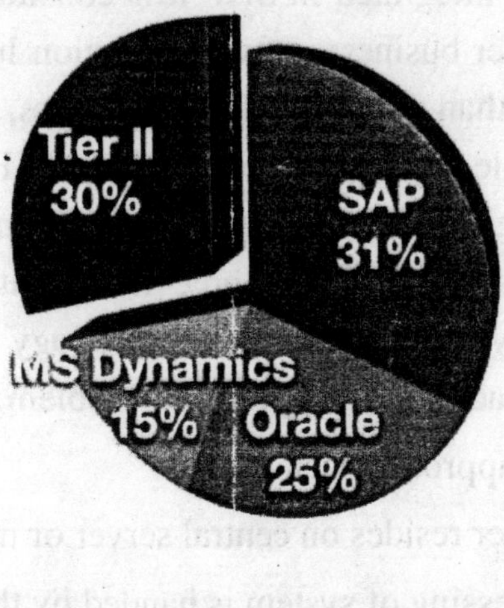

According to the chart above, SAP is still top leader with 31% market share. However, in 2005-2006, based on AMR Research, SAP market share was 47%, Oracle

25% and Microsoft was only 3%. Microsoft's market share increase from 3% to 15% while SAP's market share decrease from 47% to 31%.

SAP AG

Company Profile: SAP was founded in 1972. SAP [System Applications and Product in Data Processing].

The company is headquartered in Walldrof, Germany and the world's leading provider of client/server business application solution. Today, more than 107 countries run installation of SAP.

SAP's ERP package comes in two version, among which the main frame version (SAP R/3) is the most prominent and SAP provides customer an opportunity to install the core system, one or more of the functional components, or purchase the software as a complete package.

SAP in global market is the leading successful vendor of standard business application software and is scaled as the largest independent software supplier.

SAP continued to grow and SAP AG emerged as a publicly held corporation since 1998. In 1995 the SAP AG collaborated with DAX the index of German blue chip. SAP listed its ADRs(American Depository Receipt) on the NYSE.

Product & Technology

Due to unique feature integrated in SAP it is considered to be very sophisticated, robust incompatible by other business software solution It has broadened and extended its base now-a day more than 800 predefined business, new business processes and technology became available regularly which enables SAP customers to add state of art solution to meet ever changing business demands. SAP Software power depends in real time integration. The release of the R/3, a three–tier client server architecture was most significantly recognized by SAP customers, technology patterns and industry which appears as a winning approach in solving today's problem.

It works on 3-layered approach such as :

(1) The database layer resides on central server or main frame host computers.

(2) The logical processing of system is handed by the application layer.

(3) With the IBVs and its intensive development network all the task that typically related to personal computer are handled by presentation layer

R/3 System

SAP R/3 system is widely used in standard business for client server computer, its use increases the efficiency, flexibility. Thus around 20 lakhs customers are using this system.

Best business practices and new technologies

R/3 lets you integrative all your business operation in all overall system for planning controlling and monitoring.

Dynamic information management: Automobile manufacturing.

R/3 Modules: There are given below some R/3 modules.

- Financial Accounting
- Treasury
- Controlling
- Enterprise controlling
- Investment management
- Production planning
- Materials management
- Plant management & service management
- Quality management
- Project system
- Sales and Distribution
- Human resources management

Advantage SAP

(1) N/W optimization across all computers. R/S unlocks the client server architectures.

(2) R/S offers real time integration of solutions & it combines a variety of product & services.

(3) The application distribution & computing capability will be available across multiple levels.

BAAN

Baan is a leading global provider of Enterprise Business Software. These applications are in use at ever 7000 customers' sites worldwide. It was founded by Jan and Paul Baan in 1978 in the Netherlands.

Products manufactured by Baan company reduces complexity and cost, improve core business processes, are efficient to access and use, are more dynamic in adapting to business changes and optimize the business management of information.

Technology:

- Serving vertical industries
- Aerospace & Defense
- Automotive

Baan ERP Module

- Manufacturing Module
- Financial Module
- Project Module
- Distribution Module.

BAAN ERP Tools

(1) New market trends are quickly adapted that require flexible software configuration.

(2) Develop the BAAN application in such a way that they are kept independent of third party products such as hardware, operating system. & database.

(3) Create customers specific solution.

Run time Tools :

C, C++ and Java

- Focus on application specific issues only.
- Remove the overhead of developing and generating a native application code.
- Reduce the complexity.

Software Development Tools:

- Software configuration management
- Authorization management system
- Database management system
- Exchange from Editor
- 4 GL Program Editor

Product version

- Triton 1.0 to 2.2d, 3.0 to last version of Triton is 3.1bx, then the product is renamed to Baan
- Baan 4.0 (last version of BaanIV is BaanIVc4 SP30) & Industry extensions (A&D,...)
- Baan 5.0 (last version of BaanV is Baan5.0 c SP26)
- Baan 5.1, 5.2 (for specific customers only)
- SSA ERP 6.1 /Infor ERP LN 6.1

Oracle Corporation

Oracle Corporation is the world's 2nd largest software company founded in 1977 and it uses more than 41000 people in more than 145 countries

Technology:

- Ware house Technology Initiative (WTT)
- Business Intelligence Solutions

Application:

- Oracle Financial
- Oracle Human Resource
- Oracle Project
- Oracle Manufacturing
- Oracle Supply Chain
- Oracle Front Office.

People Soft:

To meet changing business demand of enterprise an innovative software soln. was established in 1987 with the name of people soft.

Worldwide:

Across the globe more than 7000 people prefer People Soft and in the year 1998 it contributed 1.3 billion in the annual revenue.

Business management solutions

- Human Resource Management
- Accounting And Control
- Treasury Management
- Performance Measurement
- Project Management
- Sales & Logistics
- Materials Management
- Supply Chain Planning
- Service Revenue Management
- Procurement

Commercial solutions:

- Supply Chain Management
- Service Industry Solution
- Communication Federal Government
- Finance Service
- Health Care
- Higher Education
- Manufacturing
- Retail
- Service industry
- Transpiration

- Utilities

Technology of People Soft

- Self Service Application
- Web Client
- Multitudes Transaction Processing
- Online Analytical Processing
- Work Flow

People Soft Implementation Tool Kit

- Geographical
- Departmental
- Core & Support Processes
- No Phasing
- As Delivered
- Data Modification Legacy Integration
- Application Sequential
- Business Objective And Event

JD Edwards World Solution Company

Company profile: In the year 1977 three men including Denner Colorado left the accounting would to establish a new software company that would specialize in wide range computing solutions.

Each of the great three founders are Jack Thompson, Dan Gergory & Ed Ma Vaney. This industry enlarged as the leading supplier of applications software among which IBM AS/400 is highly successful.

- Solution
- Relationship
- Value

Technology

- One world

- World software and world vision

Modules

- Foundation Suite
- Financial Suite
- Logistics/Distribution Suite
- Service Suite
- Manufacturing Suite
- Architecture, Engineering, Construction Mining & Real Estate Suite
- Energy & Chemical Suite
- Payroll Suit
- Human Resource Suit
- Customer Service Management Suite
- Government Education And Not For Profit Solution
- Utility & Energy Solutions

System software association (SSA)

In December 1981 the company was found and is headquartered in Chicago, USA. Today, SSA company run at over 2000 employees in 91 countries. Within 4000 sites of more than 1000 major industry sector firms, the company's product line BPCs client/server V, are being implemented or lived.

Key goal

- Best Client Satisfaction
- Enterprise Solution Leadership
- Enterprise Solution Leadership
- Proven Leading Technology
- Highly Skilled & Motivated Professional
- Strong Financial Result.

QAD

Company Profiles: The Company was established in 1979 and today it is widely spread in 21st countries. Today in over 80 countries and more than 4000 company have installed and it is also available in 26 different languages.

The company is certified by 1SO in 1995.

Product

Integrated supply chain management solution is provided to the MFG/PRO Software multinational organization.

Modules:

- Distribution
- Manufacturing
- Financial
- Service/Support
- Supply chain
- Master Files

Knowing the ERP Market

Analyzing ERP market share from the point of view of the market segments for any other product or services is quite different. The segmentation can be categorised in the form of many criteria like physical, geographical functionair distribution level and may more factors 3 broad categories in which ERP market segmented r (1) type of the industry (2) size of the industry (3) Geographical areas in terms of the nations where the product is demanded.

Thus these segmentation help in arriving at ERP market and ERP Software market share.

Brief detail of the segmentations are size of industry refers to its volume of business transacted & the capacity of the firm in terms of large sized or mid size or low run.

The type of industry refers to the mode of business viz. hospitality or insurance or manufacturing or health etc. thus the market form purely depends on the services offered by the render. The question of geographical segmentation involves a detailed study when it comes to ERP markets.

REVIEW QUESTIONS

1. What are the end user organization? What they are using?
2. What do you understand by ERP market?
3. In Indian content were we use ERP market?
4. What are the factor which affect the ERP market?
5. Define changing ERP market
6. Define the market players

4 ERP FUNCTIONAL MODULES

Introduction

ERP packages are distributed in number of modules and their features and number vary according to the ERP packages. In this chapter, modules that are commonly available in packages are mentioned:-

- Finance
- Sales and Distribution
- Manufacturing
- Human Resources
- Plant Maintenance
- Quality Management
- Materials Management

Finance

Information technology's concept is purely based on the fact that right information. is provided to right person at right time. Financial functionality and analysis assistance is provided by finance modules of most ERP systems to businesses. Along with financial application components, ERP also includes human resources and is linked by internet. Hundreds of business processes are taken care of in this system

The Finance Modules of most ERP systems will have the following subsystems.

(1) Financial Accounting (General Ledger, Accounts Receivable/Payable, Special Ledgers, Fixed Asset Accounting, Legal Consolidation)

(2) Investment Management (Investment Planning/Budgeting/controlling, Depreciation Forecast/Simulation/calculation)

(3) Controlling (overhead cost controlling, Activity Based Costing, Product Cost Accounting, Profitability Analysis)

(4) Treasury (Cash Management, Treasury Management, Market Risk Management, Funds Management)

(5) Enterprise Controlling (Executive Information system, Business planning & Budgeting, Profit Centre Accounting)

1. Financial Accounting: The financial accounting module of an ERP system assigns the capacity to consolidate financial accounting data within an organization, track financial data within an international framework of multiple enterprises, languages, currencies and charts of accounts

(a) **General Ledger :** For financial accounting system and strategic decision making, the general ledger is mandatory. The flexible structure of general ledger meets the functional needs of a financial accounting system.

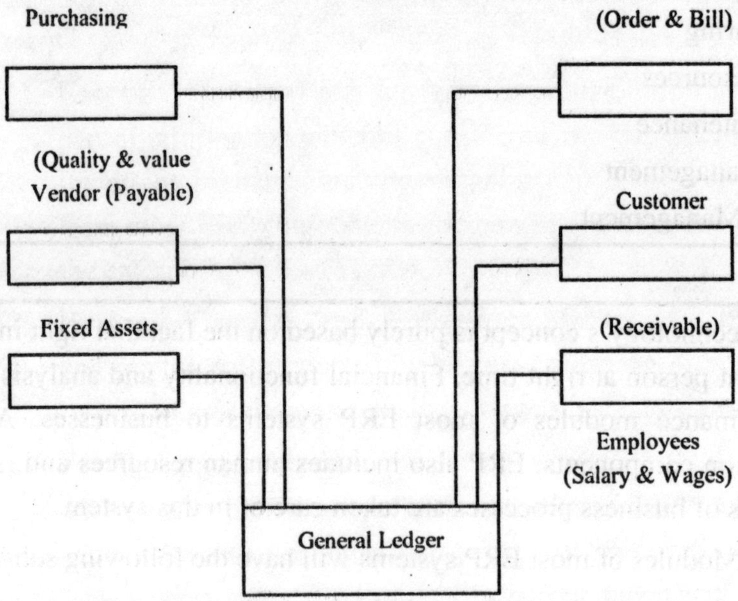

Fig. General Ledger

(b) **Accounts Receivable and Payable :** A financial overview on the matters related to global business pattern relationship in the accounts receivable & payable function can be offered by an ERP system. Thus like the general ledger these sub ledgers are also integrated along with the areas in sale and distribution and material management, where financial data originates.

(c) **Asset Accounting:** All the information of asset related transactions are accessed by the asset accounting which ultimately sources a sub-ledger to the general ledger. Company's assets are fixed within the financial accounting system through the asset accounting.

(d) **Legal Consolidation:** Consolidated financial statements need to be integrated properly with operational data at individual company level. By using different valuation methods balance sheet strategies according to organizations' need can be chalked out.

2. Investment Management: ERP planning module towards investment process are extensively supported through settlement investment management facilities, investment planning & budgeting at a level higher than that needed for specific orders or projects. The tools linked with the investment management enables you to plan and manage your capital spending projects right from the earliest stage.

(1) **Controlling:** Function related to effective internal cost accounting are gathered by the controlling system.

(1) **Overhead Cost Controlling:** Organization sometimes witnesses rapid rise in the percentage of indirect costs which cannot be directly assigned to the products manufactured.

(2) **Cost Centre Accounting:** Overheads occurring within the organization are analyzed by cost center accounting.

(3) **Overhead Orders:** Subsystems are instructed by overhead to collect & analyze costs based on individual internal measures.

(4) **Activity Based Costing:** The objective of individual department should be kept as the ultimate goal of the entire organization when it comes to business process reengineering.

3. Treasury Module: Company's success is greatly affected by treasury. Such integration also facilitates management and control of cash flows and risk positions through all the divisions in the company.

(1) **Cash Management:** The cash management is categorized as a subsystems of ERP module, it analyzes financial transactions for a

given time slot. Thus for the attainment of financial budgeting, future development records are kept, and identified by the cash management.

(2) **Treasury Management:** Treasury management deals with the task related for managing financial deals and positions from trading to transferring data to financial accounting, it also supports flexible reporting.

(3) **Market Risk Management:** Competitive environment of a company can be maintained by Market Risk Management. It also plays a vital role within Treasury.

(4) **Funds Management:** Funds management subsystem looks after the budgets, all the way through to payments including monitoring expenditures, activities and resources.

4. Enterprise Controlling: Enterprise controlling comprises of those functions that will optimize share holder value, while meeting internal objectives for growth and investment.

(1) **Executive Information System:** Executive Information system holds that part of information which is considered as a critical information and becomes important in managing the organization. This component integrates data from other ERP components and non ERP data sources both inside & outside the enterprise.

(2) **Business Planning and Budgeting:** Management teams of business units and groups are supported by business planning & budgeting departments in respect of calculation of business targets, such as returns on investment etc.

(3) **Profit Centre Accounting:** Being a part of total corporate planning, it analysis the profitability of internal responsibility centres. Basically profit centres focuses the integration aspect of corporate planning as plans from which other application areas can be combined extended & altered in this module.

Sales and Distribution

Sales and distribution module comprises of Contact Management and Sales Order Processing Management. This integrates the marketing and sales activities. By using this Module enterprises can improve sales, service and marketing effectiveness.

Sales Management module is about retaining customers, improving customer loyalty and gaining customer insight.

This helps to make get the customer order management easier day by day. Whether it is maintaining customer information, quickly creating a quote or migrating them to sales order or being responsive to the customers, this module provides the right solution and efficient flow of information.

The following are the sales related business transactions which includes sales queries, such as inquiries and quotations. This also includes-

- Sales orders
- Outline agreements such as contracts
- Delivery/Shipment
- Invoicing/Billing
- After sales support

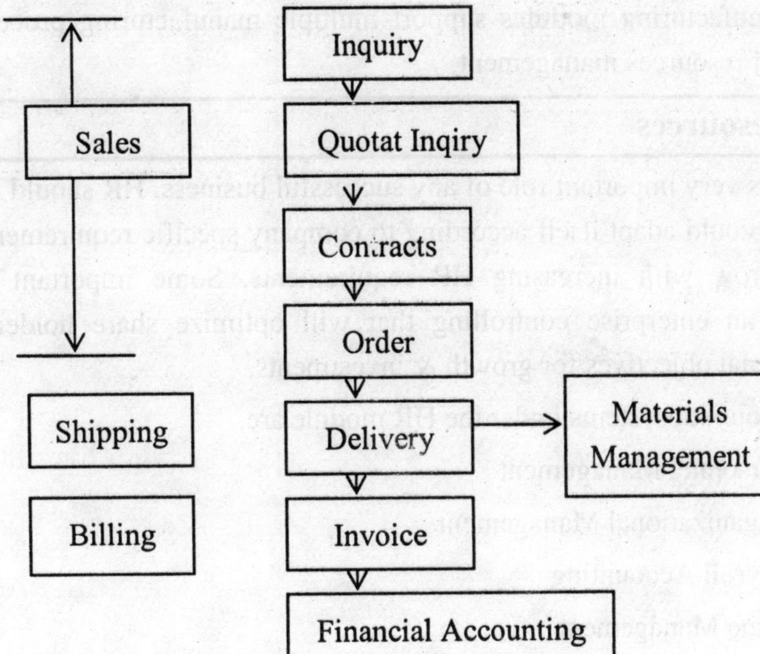

The sales & distribution module

Fig above shows sales Distribution & its associated processes Typically, a sales & distribution module will contain the following subsystems.

(1) Master Data Management

(2) Order Management

(3) Warehouse Management

(4) Shipping

(5) Billing

(6) Pricing

(7) Sales Support

(8) Transportation

(9) Foreign Trade

Manufacturing

The manufacturing modules support multiple manufacturing processes with full integration of resources management.

Human Resources

HR plays very important role of any successful business. HR should be designed in a way that it could adapt itself according to company specific requirements and should constantly grow with increasing HR requirements. Some important functions are included in an enterprise controlling that will optimize share holder value while meeting internal objectives for growth & investments.

The various subsystems under the HR module are.

(1) Personnel Management

(2) Organizational Management

(3) Payroll Accounting

(4) Time Management

Plant Maintenance

The Plant Maintenance module in ERP provides an integrated solution for technical and business reports and various presentation options, according to the criteria used in plant maintenance and manufacturing units: for example organizational unit, location, execution period for tasks, or system manufacturer. This information helps to reduce the duration and costs of plant breakdown times due to damage and to recognize possible weak points within the technical system during good time.

The major sub-systems of an ERP Plant & Machine Maintenance module are:

- Breakdown Repair Log
- Equipment Master Register
- Machine Breakdown Log
- Maintenance Type
- Man Power for Machine Details
- Preventive Maintenance Record
- Spare Part Installation Log

Quality Management

The quality management functions and elements are defined by the ISO 9000 series of standardization. The elements which are supported by the functions of quality management modules are:

(1) Quality Planning

(2) Quality Inspection

(3) Quality Control

Materials Management

The materials management module optimizes all purchasing processes with workflow driven processing functions which automatically enables supplier evaluation and warehousing costs with accurate inventory and warehouse management. The main modules of the materials management are:

(1) Repurchasing activities

(2) Purchasing

(3) Vendor evaluation

(4) Inventory management

(5) Invoice verification and material inspection.

ERP Integration

ERP combines multiple data sources and processes into a streamlined system as a result of which now-a-days many organization are specialized in ERP system development due to high costs of ERP development.

ERP software constructs modular products, so that they can be easily deployed. Few modules such as accounting and finance are commonly used in many organization but modules like SCM & manufacturing may not be acquired by all organization.

ERP integration is an expensive, complicated and time consuming process. Therefore usually it is implemented as a three step process such as:

(1) Consultation

(2) Implementation and

(3) Support

Consultation

Before adopting ERP in business, it is must for an organization to seek an expert advice from someone who can give a clear idea on the disadvantages of existing solution which the organization thinks has a long term benefits. ERP consultation costs vary greatly depending on the complexity of the project, the resources & allocated budget & time for instance-a large in scale manufacturing organization may take years to implement as compared to a small scale enterprise. It can go through this process within a week.

Implementation

Another step of ERP integration is implementation. It is the most complex stage, since a system is implemented only after considering many consultation firms about a system's history & background. Despite of being a complex system, few of them are customized to support legacy database & software. Transferring a data to the new system, so that the organization can gain the maximum benefits of the ERP system is always regarded as a wise decision.

Time span of an implementation phase vary from two to three months to about two years depending on the project complexity. HR are another aspect in ERP integration. This process can be picked up by any organization or a specialized organization.

ERP integration projects which are carried out on large scale generally chooses to train or hire their own employees which therefore has two benefits.

(1) Having their staff reduces costs & provides technical in house expertise.

(2) Due to the presence of own employees, the organization will be able to feel more confident and can have better understanding of the existing business processes.

However the ultimate solution is to adopt an hybrid implementation, which means specialized staff working along with in house staff.

Support

Integration phase is followed by the support phase and supporting an ERP system is one of the crucial decisions an organization has to make because of its effect on the TCO (**Total Cost Of Ownership**). Few of the expenditure areas that might be considered are in house & external staffing, staff hiring, infrastructure & software vendor fees. But for small scale projects in house staff can be trained, and for a large scale ERP integration projects a dedicated team is required.

ERP Integration Issues

Apart from careful planning, consultations & implementation an ERP Integration faces some major challenges like:

1. Balance between the existing business processes and the standardized solution offered by the ERP software vendor.
2. For a faster system deployment an organization will have to amend some of the existing rules, so that the implementation teams must work closely with the core business decision makers to let them know that they do not lose their competitive advantages during the process.
3. Due to data migration strategy which includes to migrate data & eliminate those legacy systems ultimately leads to one of the issues in ERP integration that might arise is the data & system compatibility with legacy system.

Thorough & careful planning is required for ERP Integration which may require weeks to years for implementation, with experienced consultation implementation and support ERP can amplify the competitive advantage of a company.

ERP software integration involves meeting various B2B demands by integrating separate ERP systems with each other or with other enterprise information resources. The main objective of constructing an ERP system such as SAP, PeopleSoft, and

Oracle etc. is tightly integrating the processes within as enterprise. An ERP software product encompasses to include planning manufacturing, sales, marketing, inventory control, order tracking, customer services, finance and human resources as a main tool.

Top Problems Involved in ERP Integration

Integration of projects sometimes works differently from the planned structure. For instance the time slot decided for implementing project may not fit to that of the concerned department. Apart from this some serious problems related with the aim of integrating the ERP system, reducing staffing after full implementation and providing sufficient return on investment so that breakeven is achieved in 3 years and profit in 4 years, will definitely required a good preset plan that would look forward to realizing possible consideration measure to tackle problems that may occur when the project is on progress.

The following the top 5 problems involved in ERP Integration.

1. Problem arise due to miscommunication if information at various levels of project, like at the project manager's level, the project director can wrongly perceive the project scheduling, further the senior ERP Integration Project Manager get wrong information from Project Director on the time to be taken for implementation.
2. The following are reasons which can support the delay of the project.
   (*a*) Pending/Due of the ERP software
   (*b*) Untrained staff members
   (*c*) Lack of identification of the requirements in integration process.
   (*d*) Over optimistic nature of cost position in ERP integration
   (*e*) The known amendments are quiet extensive.
3. The major role in project objective is played by the ERP software vendor, but somehow due to lack of co-ordination between ERP software vendor and organization, may lead to the incorrect evaluation of the ERP software, its acquisition and subsequent enhancement & its integration in user premises & maintenance will again become a bog problem.

This drawback can prove to be more dangerous when no pre-planned software suppliers list are kept with the organization to meet the prior commencement of the project.

4. The first person to encounter the problem in ERP software acquisition is the system analyst. Three major concerns that can be possibly associated to the acquired ERP software system are
   (*a*) The organization needs to implement a board to allow the ERP integration that would cause additional expenditure to the project.
   (*b*) Breakdown of ERP software and each day within the week a new evaluation model should be created by an engineer.
5. If the organization becomes too result oriented & fascinated by the ERP software's ability to enable the effective management of their resources notwithstanding the problems to be anticipated before committing to the ERP software supplier thus gives an outlook of taking a fatalistic notion of committing to the project which could ultimately spells to bring a trouble in the ERP integration

Success to the organization is needed but if it is based on smooth moving and proper planning the failures of any organization the most obvious missing reason can be stated is the positive & definite integration plan that would have anticipated the drawbacks mentioned along with corresponding actions on the anticipated problems. Hence by acquiring this way, the possible setback on ERP integration mentioned above will never happen.

5 ERP IMPLEMENTATION LIFE CYCLE

ERP Implementation

The implementation of an ERP project starts with a clear view of determining objectives. The objectives includes characteristics are-

(i) Speed

(ii) Scope

(iii) Resource

(iv) Risk

(v) Complexity

(vi) Benefits

1. Speed: speeds depend on the time span that the company would like to take for the implementation or in other words it is the amount of time the company is considering for implementing the system which could dramatically differ.

2. Scope: The scope of the projects depends on various types of functional and technical characteristics that tlie company wants to implement.

3. Resources: To support any project, resources are everything and various resources hold one thing in common i.e. "money":

(i) People

(ii) Hardware System

(iii) Software System

(iv) Technical Support and

(v) Consultant.

4. Risk: The risk of project has great impact on the entire success o the ERP implementation. The criteria on which the success measured are overall user acceptance, ROI(return on investment), time to implement etc.

5. Complexity: Complexity is the degree of difficulty of:

(i) Implementing

(ii) Operating and

(iii) Maintaining the ERP System.

Level of complexity varies according to the companies of different size, business environments and organization culture.

Complexity in a multinational company is generally much more than small company. For example, production team of a MNC may be spread across different parts of the world and working in different time zone.

6. Benefits: To extend the functionality of ERP system for software development, maintenance and other support activities, the benefits are utilized by the company. The organization activities are automated by the ERP tools to make the job of the employee, managers and other stakeholders easy and improve the development and productivity.

Better integration of the ERP system along with the software development and the maintenance process will result in high quality products, reduction in the number of defects, quicker incorporation of enhancement, better customer services and support etc.

ERP implementation project passes through various levels of phases without indicating border line of completion as in many cases, one phase starts earlier than the previous one is completed but the order followed is logical:

The different phases of the ERP implementation are given below:

1. Pre-Evaluation Screening
2. Package Evaluation
3. Project Planning Phase
4. Gap Analysis
5. Reengineering
6. Configuration
7. Implementation Team Training

8. Testing
9. Going Live
10. End Uses Training
11. Post Implementation

1. Pre-valuation screening:

By consulting a number of vendors decision for perfect package selection is done. This process eliminates those packages which is not suitable company's business process.

2. Package evaluation: One of the most important phases that will decide the success or failure of the ERP implementation project is the evaluation process.

Some important points to be kept in mind while evaluating ERP software include.

Various parameters are taken care of while selecting the package:

1. Test and certify the package, and find out the coordination amongst different departments.
2. Selected package will determine the success and failure of the project
3. User-friendliness of the package
4. Complexity and scalability
5. Regular upgradation is available or not
6. Ability to support multi site planning and control
7. Technology client/server capabilities
8. cost factor, including license and training cost

3. Project planning phase: This is the phase that designs the implementation process. Planning of how to go about the implementation is decided by a committee constituted by the team leaders of each implementation group. The committee is headed by the ERP in-charge. The committee will meet periodically to review the progress and chart the future courses of actions. In this process resources available are also identified.

4. Gap Analysis: in this a model is created to find out the gap between the current status and the future goal, i.e.., where they currently stand and where they want to head, is decided. This helps to avoid the functional gaps in the organization.

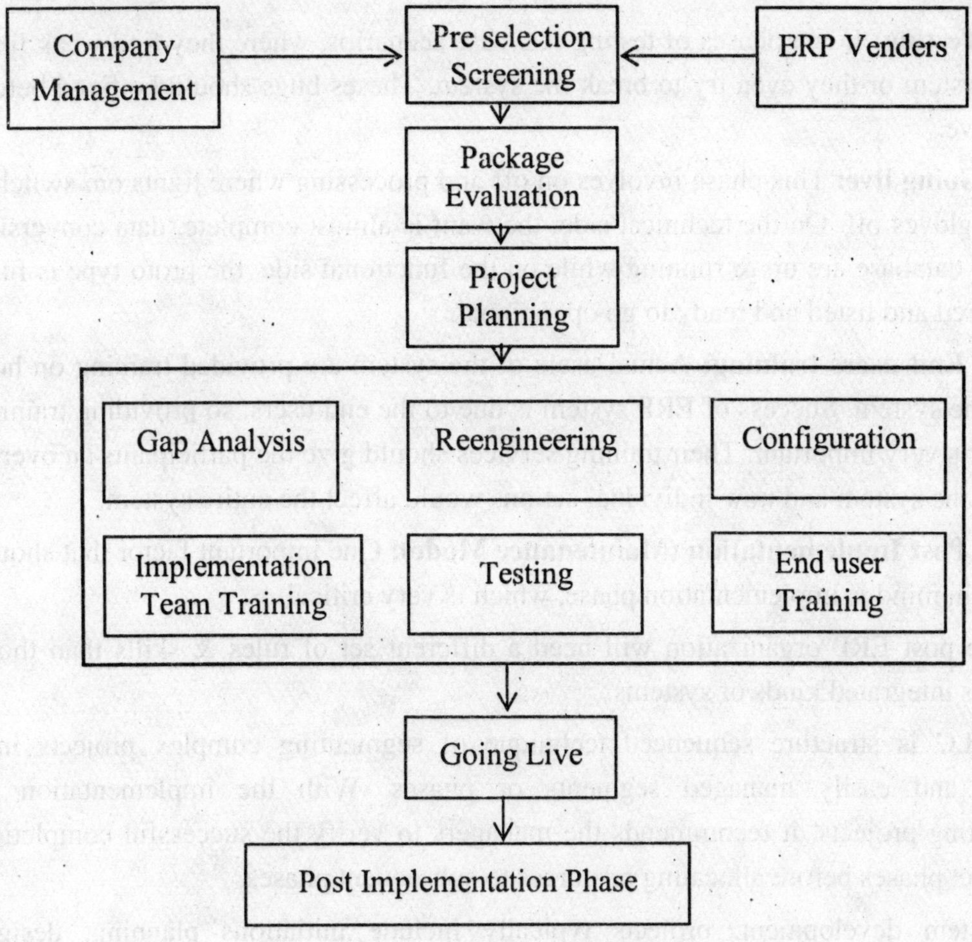

ERP Implementation Lifecycle different phases

5. Re-engineering: Re-engineering is conducted with two different arguments. first takes care of the human factors and the second on the usage, jobs and training needs. Thus second is more focused on re-engineering.

6. Configuration: The next most important functional area of ERP implementation is configuring which reveals not only the strengths of a company's business processes but also its weaknesses.

7. Implementation team training: It takes place simultaneously with the configuration process. It is a phase where company trains its employees not only how to use the system but also to implement it and later run the system.

8. Testing: It is a phases of testing real case scenarios, where they find weak links in the system or they even try to break the system. Theses bugs should be fixed before going live.

9. Going live: This phase involves on off and processing where lights on, switches thrown gloves off. On the technical side, the want is almost complete, data conversion is done, database are up & running while on the functional side, the proto type is fully configured and listed and ready to go operational.

10. End users training: Actual users of the system are provided training on how to use the system. Success of ERP system is due to the end users, so providing training to them is very important. Their training services should give the participants an overall view of the system and now individual actions would affect the entire system.

11. Post Implementation (Maintenance Mode): One important factor that should be kept in mind is implementation phase, which is very critical.

The post ERP organization will need a different set of rules & skills than those with less integrated kinds of systems.

SDLC is structure sequenced technique of segmenting complex projects into smaller and easily managed segments or phases. With the implementation of segmenting projects, it recommends the managers to verify the successful completion of project phases before allocating resources to subsequent phases.

System development. projects typically include initiations planning, design, development, testing, implementation, and maintenance, moreover the division of these phases are done on the basis of organization involved. For instance – initial project activities might be designated as request requirements, definition, and planning phases, or initiation, concept development and planning phases. Thus the end users of the system under development should be provided the duty by reviewing each phase to ensure the system is being built to deliver the needed functionality.

Initiation Phase

Projects should be effectively analyzed & accessed to support strategic business objectives and resources are effectively implemented into an organization enterprise architecture. This phase starts up by getting the opportunity to add, improve, or correct a system, it is identified and formally requested through the presentation of a business case. The business case should at least describe a proposals purpose, identify expected benefits, and explain how the proposed system cater to the organization's business strategies along with identifying alternative solution. Projects are rejected or accepted on the basis of presentation of a business case before they allocate resources to formal feasibility study. This depends on the desired request, subsequent feasibility of evaluating software development and management should consider input and output from all affected parties. Management should also closely evaluate the necessity of each requested functional requirement. Various design documents and hundreds of lines of code are included as a single software feature in initiation phase. It can also maximize testing, documentation and support requirements. Rejected features reduces the resources required to completes a project.

The initial point of feasibility study passes through the request documentation which requires management to verify the accuracy of the preliminary assumptions and identify requirement of resources in greater detail.

- **Business Considerations:**
  - Strategic business and technology goals and objectives;
  - Expected benefits measured against the value of current technology;
  - Potential organizational changes regarding facilities or the addition/reduction of end users, technicians, or managers;
  - Budget, scheduling, or personnel constraints; and
  - Potential business, regulatory, or legal issues that could impact the feasibility of the project.
- **Functional Requirements:**
  - End-user functional requirements;
  - Internal control and information security requirements;
  - Operating, database, and backup system requirements (type, capacity, performance);
  - Connectivity requirements (stand-alone, Local Area Network, Wide Area Network, external);
  - Network support requirements (number of potential users; type, volume, and

frequency of data transfers); and

- Interface requirements (internal or external applications).

◆ **Project Factors:**

- Project management methodology;
- Risk management methodology;
- Estimated completion dates of projects and major project phases; and
- Estimated costs of projects and major project phases.

◆ **Cost/Benefit Analysis:**

- Expected useful life of the proposed product;
- Alternative solutions (buy vs. build);
- Nonrecurring project costs (personnel, hardware, software, and overhead);
- Recurring operational costs (personnel, maintenance, telecommunications, and overhead);
- Tangible benefits (increased revenues, decreased costs, return-on-investments); and
- Intangible benefits (improved public opinions or more useful information).

The feasibility support documentation is a layout of the proposed project and identify expected costs and benefits in terms of economic, technical and operational feasibility describes alternative solutions and needs a recommendation for approval or rejection. The documents compiled and submitted are reviewed and signed off in by all affected parties, then used for senior management or board study and if approved, management should use the feasibility study and support documentation to start the planning phase.

Planning Phase

In finishing development, acquisition, and maintenance project, planning phase plays a very important role to coordinate activities and manage project risks effectively particularly in the early stages of a project. The depth and formality of projects plans should be communicate with the characteristics and risks of a given project.

Review the planning phase, information gathered during the initiation phase are refined by further recognizing the specific activities and resources required to complete a project. A critical part of a project manager's job is to coordinate discussions between user, audit, security, design, development and network personal to identify and document as many functional, security and network requirements as possible.

Primary items organization should address in formal project plans include:

- **Project overview:** Project overview is a layout of the project plan, which should identify the project, project sponsors, project managers, project description, goals background information. and development strategies.
- **Roles and responsibilities:** It define the key personnel responsibility such as project sponsors, managers and team members, third party venders responsibility and internal audit, security and network personnel.
- **Communication:** Due to defined communication techniques project efficiencies are maximized therefore management should establish procedures for gathering and dissemination information. such as standard report, forms, defined reporting requirements, established meeting schedules, which facilitates project communication and acceptance criteria for each project phase. It should also maintain appropriate review and approval procedures to ensure project teams complete all phases, before moving into subsequent phases.
- **Defined deliverables:** For successfully winding the project, it should be explaining natural project objectives, accurate informational, functional and interface requirements and objective acceptance criteria.
- **Control Requirements:** Redesigning and building automated control and security are the essential features of the planning phase thus their recognition to place them during initial project phase is a difficult task however control issues and security for those features in application should be considered by management during a project's life cycle.
- **Risk Management:** For organization, risk assessment, monitoring and managing internal and external risks is an important task throughout the project's life cycle. The procedures should include risk acceptance, initiation, and transfer strategies.

External risk issues are :-

- Vendor failure
- Regulatory changes.
- Natural disasters

While internal risks issues are:

- Budgets, such as in accurate cost forecasting or changing functional requirements,
- Scheduling difficulties, such as unexpected personnel changes or inaccurate development assumptions
- Work flow challenges such as weak communication or in experienced project managers & change management.

Software development projects on the request of personnel are often added or modified on the bases of functional requirements that may be exact, standard should be in place to control changes in order to minimize disruptions to the development process. According to the changes needed, the project manager should establish deadlines and employees of same department should be involved in evaluating and approving proposed changes. Large, complex, or mission critical projects should include formal change management procedures.

Standards: Application standards such as project oversight activities, system controls and quality assurance should be considered by project plans. Oversight standards should address project methodology selections, approval authorities and risk management procedures System control standard should address functional, security and automated control requirements. Quality assurance standards should address the validity of project assumptions, adherence to project standards and testing of a product's overall performance. The following standards should be reviewed, approved and document deviations by the management.

- **Documentation:** The category and status of documentation personnel should be recognized by project plan. For instance during the initiation phase personnel should document project objectives, system requirements, and development strategies. Revision procedure of documentation i.e. preliminary user, operator, and maintenance manuals created during the design phase should be revision during development and testing phases while finalized during the implementation phase.

- **Scheduling:** Each major project phase should be scheduled before performing any tasks by the management. Flexibility into project schedule should be initiated to tackle any uncertainties. However with the success of project, amount of flexibility declines and requirements become more defined.
- **Budget:** Feasibility of project is determined by overall project costs which are monitored carefully and adjusted if needed by the managers however, they should return a baseline budget for post project analysis. Additional expenses and outsourcing activities should be associated with project overheads such as office space, between & software used during the project.
- **Testing:** Management that included users, designs, developers and system technicians should be involved to identify testing requirements and schedule testing procedures throughout the initial phases of a project.
- **Staff development:** Employees should be benefited by participating in plans that identify testing requirements and schedule training procedures to use and maintain an application after implementation.

Design Phase

Initiation and planning phase is further followed by design phase that convert the informational, functional and network requirements into unified design specifications that developers use to script programs during the development phase. Numerous methods are used to constrict program designs. Using a top-down approach designers first identify and link major program components and interfaces then expand design layouts as they identify and link smaller subsystems and connection while in using bottom-up approach, designers first identify and link minor program components and interfaces, then expand design layouts as they identify and link larger systems and connections.

Prototyping tools are used for constructing mock-up designs of items such as application screens, database layouts and system architectures in contemporary design techniques. On iterative bases prototyped design are reviewed and refund by the end user, designers, developers database managers, and network administrators while audit, security and quality assurances personnel is also involved in it.

Prototyping techniques accelerated an organization capacity to design and establish controls i.e. to develop automated controls, management should be particularly diligent. However, employees may be included to resist adding additional controls, even though they are needed after the initial designs are established.

Designers should completely analyze the detailed document, design to develop programs and modify them after they placed in production. The documentation also helps management ensure final programs are consistent with original goal and specification.

Organization should create initial testing, conversion, and implementation and training plans during the design phase in addition they should draft user, operation and maintenance manuals.

Application Control Standards

Application controls are performed automatically by the systems, designed to ensure the complete and accurate processing of data, from input through output. These controls differ from business to business on their specific applications. These controls also help guarantees privacy and security of data transmitted between applications

Input Controls

Controls that ensure data integrity input from upstream sources into the application system. Few examples are mentioned below:

- **Check Digits:** Check digits are numbers produced by mathematical calculations performed on input data such as account numbers. The calculation confirms the accuracy of input by verifying the calculated number against other data in the input data, typically the final digit.
- **Completeness Checks:** Completeness checks confirm that blank fields are not input and that cumulative input matches control totals.
- **Duplication Checks:** Duplication checks confirm that duplicate information is not input.
- **Limit Checks:** Limit checks confirm that a value does not exceed predefined limits.

- **Range Checks:** Range checks confirm that a value is within a predefined range of parameters.
- **Reasonableness Checks:** Reasonableness checks confirm that a value meets predefined criteria.
- **Sequence Checks:** Sequence checks confirm that a value is sequentially input or processed.
- **Validity Checks:** Validity checks confirm that a value conforms to valid input criteria.

Processing Controls

With the help of automated input output controls employees would accurately ensure I/P information, system properly record I/P and systems either reject or accept and record, I/P and systems either reject or accept and record, I/P errors for later review and correction. The application involved in processing controls are merging files, modifying data, updating master files and performing files maintenance. Few examples are mentioned below:

- **Batch Controls:** Batch controls verify processed run totals against input control totals. Batches are verified against various items such as total dollars, items, or documents processed.
- **Error Reporting:** Error reports identify items or batches that include errors. Items or batches with errors are withheld from processing, posted to a suspense account until corrected, or processed and flagged for later correction.
- **Transaction Logs:** Users verify logged transactions against source documents. Administrators use transaction logs to track errors, user actions, resource usage, and unauthorized access.
- **Run-to-Run Totals:** Run-to-run totals compiled during input, processing, and output stages are verified against each other.
- **Sequence Checks:** Sequence checks identify or reject missing or duplicate entries.
- **Interim Files:** Operators revert to automatically created interim files to validate the accuracy, validity, and completeness of processed data.

- **Backup Files:** Operators revert to automatically created master-file backups if transaction processing corrupts the master file.

Output Controls

System security and processed information is distribution by automated O/P controls. Examples of automated O/P controls include.

- **Batch Logs:** Batch totals O/P are recorded and recipients distribute the verified O/P of batch logs.
- **Distribution Controls:** Only authorised individuals protect distribution controls. Automated distribution lists and access restrictions on information. stored electronically on spooled to printers are examples of distribution controls.
- **Destruction Controls:** Destruction controls help ensure electronically distributed and due to overvaulting outdated information or demagnetizing (degassing) disks and tapes all the stored information is destroyed.

Development Phase

The development phase helps to convent design specification into executable programs and such requirement are discussed by design specifications before programming begins for effective development standards. The procedures help to ensure programmers clearly understand program designs and functional requirements.

Procedural programming is a programming technique which involves line by line scripting of logical instructions that are combined to form a program which is based upon the concept of the procedure call like routines, subroutines, methods, or functions etc. These are used by programs requiring large transactions like financial calculations.

The tools for creating and testing a primary procedural programming activities and the refinement and finalization of test plans, small routines programs that carry out particular task within an application is prepared by individual programmers, known as desk test program models or components. Completed components are integrated with other components and reviewed often by a group of programmers, to ensure the components properly interact. The process continues as component groups are progressively integrated and tested.

Object-oriented programming is an advanced programming techniques which is based on program routines (modules) classification of data types (number, letters, dollars etc.) and data structures (records, files, tables, etc.)

For the ease to modify and to reduce development times the predefined data class objects are linked in pre-scripted modules..

Organization should complete testing plans, update conversion, implementation and training plans, operation and maintenance manuals during the development phase.

Development Standards

Software Development Standards are the group of activity which ensures quality software to be developed. This is done by standardized methods and procedures laid down by government, institutions etc..

The software development process needs to follow a methodology suitable for the specific software under consideration and acceptable for a specific project. The development of this software is established and described by a Software Development Plan.

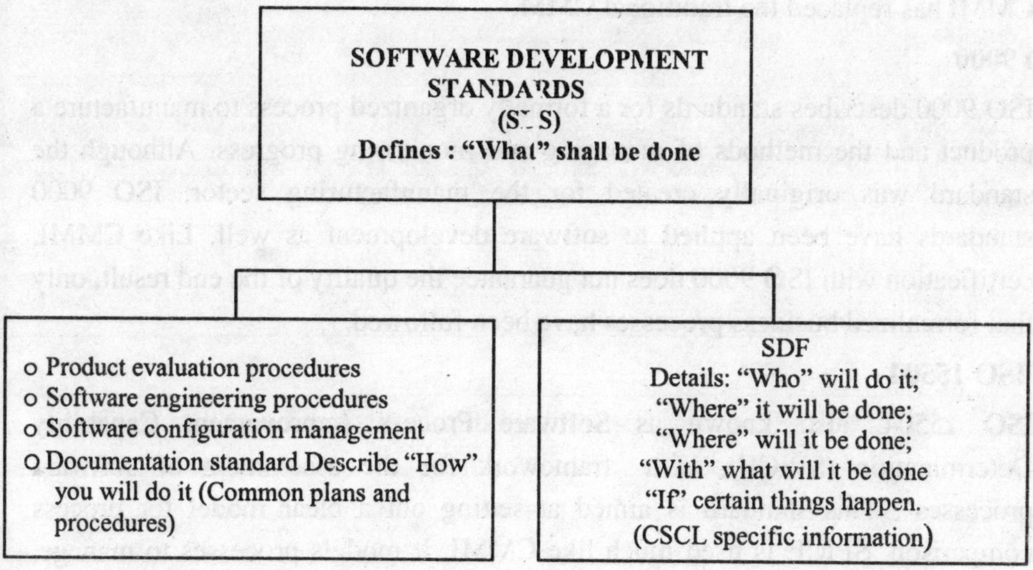

The Software Development Standards and supporting plans are prepared by the Software Management Group (SMG) who enforce, maintain, improve the system on a continuous basis.

Proposed "Software Management" documentation is known as the "Software Development Standards" which comprises of:

- Software Development Standard;
- Software Development Plan (overall); when applicable
- Software Configuration Management Plan;
- Software Product Evaluation Plan;
- Software Engineering Manual;
- Software Documentation Standard;
- Software Safety Aspects; when applicable

UNIVERSALLY AGREED STANDARDS

Capability Maturity Model Integration

The Capability Maturity Model Integration (CMMI) is one of the leading models of application development standards. It is based on independently assessing and grading the organizations on how well they follow their defined processes and not on the quality of those processes or the software produced. CMMI has replaced the traditional CMM.

ISO 9000

ISO 9000 describes standards for a formally organized process to manufacture a product and the methods of managing and monitoring progress. Although the standard was originally created for the manufacturing sector, ISO 9000 standards have been applied to software development as well. Like CMMI, certification with ISO 9000 does not guarantee the quality of the end result, only that formalized business processes have been followed.

ISO 15504

ISO 15504, also known as Software Process Improvement Capability Determination (SPICE), is a "framework for the assessment of software processes". This standard is aimed at setting out a clear model for process comparison. SPICE is used much like CMMI. It models processes to manage, control, guide and monitor software development. This model is then used to measure what a development organization or project team actually does during software development. This information is analyzed to identify weaknesses and drive improvement. It also identifies strengths that can be continued or integrated into common practice for that organization or team.

Library Controls

Stored documentation of programs and data are assembled together to form libraries. Resizable program routines or modules stored in source or object code format into the program libraries. Program libraries allow programmers to access frequently used routines and implement to programs without having to rewrite the code. Dynamic link libraries include executable code program that can be automatically run as part of larger applications

Version Controls

Library controls facilitate software version controls. Version controls provide a means to systematically retain chronological copies of revised programs and program documentation.

Version control is also referred to as concurrent version system. This is used for tracking the different versions of the software during the development process. Systems are capable in maintaining one file and identify and store only changed code. While the multiple version of source code files are not identified and stored by the system. On the requirement of the user versions are recreated. Concurrent version systems facilitate the quick identification of version and also facilitate the quick identification of programming errors. For instance if programmers install a revised program as a test server and discover programming errors, they only have to review the changed code to identify the errors.

Software Documentation

Detailed documentation should be maintained by organization for each application and application system in production, which enhances an organization's ability to understand functional, security and control features. It also helps improves the ability to use and maintain the software.

Components of documentation are detailed application descriptions, programming documentation and operation instructions. To achieve the required documentation, standards should be in place that identifies the type and format such as system narratives, flowcharts and any special system. Coding internal controls or layouts not known within individual application documentation.

In two ways management should maintain documentation i.e. for internally developed programs and externally acquired products. In case of acquired software management should ensure (either through an internal review or third party certification) prior to purchase that an acquired products documentation meets their organization's minimum documentation standards.

During the execution of documentation activities, examiner should consider access and change controls which help to ensure organization appropriately approval, test & record software modifications. Access controls access to sections of documentation that directly relates to their job function of individuals.

System documentation should include:

- **System Descriptions:** System description provides narrative explanation of operating environments and the interrelated input, processing, and output functions of integrated application systems.
- **System Documentation:** System documentation includes system flowcharts and models that identify the source and type of input information, processing and control actions (automated and manual), and the nature and location of output information.
- **System File Layouts:** System file layouts describe collections of related records generated by individual processing applications. For example, personnel may need system file layouts to describe interim files, such as sorted deposit transaction files, in order to further define master file processing requirements.

Application documentation should include:

- **Application Description:** Descriptive explanations of an application and provides overviews of data input, processing and output function.
- **Layouts:** Layouts represent the format of stared and viewed information such as database layouts, screen displays and hardcopy information.
- **Program Documentation:** Specific details of data, processing, O/P instructions, system security are included in program documentation. It mostly contains program listing source code and related narrative comments thereby consist of technical programming scripts & non-technical description of the

script listing and consent documentation is updated and modified by developers. Many software development tools are available that automatically creates source listing and narrative descriptions.

Traditionally, designers and developers have used flow charts to present pictorial views in sequencing of procedural programs such as COBOL. Flow charts provide a practical way to illustrate complex programs. The availability of flowchart software can automatically chart programs or enable programmers to chart programs dynamically without the need to draw them manually.

Object oriented programming technique have contributed to the use of dynamic flowcharting products and also help in maintaining detailed documentation of object oriented code which provides a primary benefit of the programming techniques in the reuse of program object.

- **Naming conventions:** The most risky task performed in a program documentation is naming conventions. Which are comprised of many lines of code, generally arranged hierarchically into small groups of code (modules, subroutines, or components), that perform individual functions within an application. Programmers are assigned the role to name and document the modules and any related subroutines, database, or programs that interact within an application. Standardized naming conventions, allow programmers to link subroutines into a unified programs and facilitate technicians and programmer's ability to understand & modify programs.
- **Operation Instruction:** With respect to all processing applications, the organizations should establish operator instructions. The duty of guides is to deliver operators how to perform particular jobs & how to respond to system requisites or interrupts. The documentation should only include information related to the computer operation function. An operation cannot access program documentation such as source listing record layouts and program flow charts operator instruction should be so clear to the unfamiliar operator that he can easily assist it without the help of an experienced operator.
- **End user Instructions:** Organization should establish end user instructions that describes how to use an application, operation manuals, or online help features, and system error messages. These are forms of instruction that assist individuals in using application and responding to their queries.

Testing Phase

Organizations test the accuracy of programmed code on various parameters to ensure, the inclusion of expected functionality, and the interoperability of application and other network components. It is really difficult to meet organization need and end user requirements. If organization opts effective project management techniques, then they will complete test plans and would develop applications, before entering into the testing phase. In case, project management techniques or demands are weaker then the organization may come under pressure to develop test plans at the starting of the testing phase. Test plans created during initial project phases enhances an organization's ability to create detailed tests and could significantly increases user plans into which that testers will identify weaknesses before products are implemented.

Testing groups are categorized into technicians and end users who are responsible for assembling and loading representative tests data into a testing environment. Each group performs their test in respective stages, either from a top down or bottom up approach.

A bottom up approach starts by testing smaller components and they proceed to add and tests additional components and systems. A top dawn approach starts by testing major comments and proceeds to smaller components and connections. The progression and definitions of completed tests vary between organizations.

Bottom-up tests often begin with functional (requirement based) testing. Functional tests ensure that expected functional, security and internal control features exist and operated accurately. Complete integration and end-to-end testing is done by testers so that application and system components could interact properly. Users then conduct acceptance tests to ensure system meet defined acceptance criteria.

Program drawbacks are identified by testers during the testing phase. Procedures should be appropriately placed before the programmers to correct defects and document all corrections or modifications. As the problems are corrected efficiency of testing phase increases and it also saves time in debugging. Documenting correction and modification is necessary to maintain the integrity of the overall program documentation.

Organizations should review and complete user, operator, and maintenance manuals during the testing phase. Additionally, they should finalize conversion, implementation, and training plans.

Primary tests include:

- **Acceptance Testing:** End users perform acceptance tests to assess the overall functionality and interoperability of an application.
- **End-to-End Testing:** End users and system technicians perform end-to-end tests to assess the interoperability of an application and other system components such as databases, hardware, software, or communication devices.
- **Functional Testing:** End users perform functional tests to assess the operability of a program against predefined requirements. Functional tests include black box tests, which assess the operational functionality of a feature against predefined expectations, or white box tests, which assess the functionality of a feature's code.
- **Integration Testing:** End users and system technicians perform integration tests to assess the interfaces of integrated software components.
- **Parallel Testing:** End users perform parallel tests to compare the output of a new application against a similar, often the original, application.
- **Regression Testing:** End users retest applications to assess functionality after programmers make code changes to previously tested applications.
- **Stress Testing:** Technicians perform stress tests to assess the maximum limits of an application.
- **String Testing:** Programmers perform string tests to assess the functionality of related code modules.
- **System Testing:** Technicians perform system tests to assess the functionality of an entire system.
- **Unit Testing:** Programmers perform unit tests to assess the functionality of small modules of code.

Implementation Phase

Installation of approved application into production environment is included in the implementation phase. Primary task involve training end users, announcing the implementation schedule and installing the product. In addition organization should enter & establish truth data or correct data, configure and test system and security parameters and conduct post implementation reviews. It is the duty of management that they should pass on the implementation schedules amongst all the users of the system and should inform if any implementation related work has to be done.

Pre-existing data is manually entered or electronically transferred to new system after installation of product by organization. Correcting the accuracy of the input data & security configurations is a most difficult part of the implementation process. After varying the accuracy and reliability of the new system organization run a new system in parallel with an old system. During the verification process employees document any programming, procedural, or configuration changes.

Project Evaluation

For the validation of the completion of project objectives and assessing project management activities, management should have post implementation review at the end of a project. All the personnel are involved by management so that the operational use of the product and document, and address any identified problem.

Effectiveness of project management activities is analyzed by the management by making comparison amongst planned and actual cost and retrieved benefit from the development before the senior management, they should present the document of results.

Maintenance Phase

To help its operational effectiveness, maintenance phase involve making changes to hardware, software & documentation. It also includes making changes to make better system performance. Correct problems, enhance security, or address user requirements. To make certain or safe modification it is not advisable to interrupt operations or degrade a system's performance or security. Correct change management standard and procedures are established by an organization.

All aspects of an organization's technology environment should address by change controls which involve software program, hardware and software configurations, operation standard & procedures and project management activities. For addressing major, routine, emergency modification there should be establishment of change control by management and crucial modification involve significant changes to a system's functionality. By using SDLC methodology, process management should enact major modification by using this well-structured process. Major modification is most complex then Routine changes. Routine change control should involve procedures for requesting, evaluating, approving, testing, installing & documentation software modification.

Routine changes are not as complex as major modifications and can usually be implemented in the normal course of business. Routine change controls should include procedures for requesting, evaluating, approving, testing, installing, and documenting software modifications.

Emergency changes may address an issue that would normally be considered routine, however, because of security concerns or processing problems, the changes must be made quickly. Emergency change controls should include the same procedures as routine change controls. Management should establish abbreviated request, evaluation, and approval procedures to ensure they can implement changes quickly. Detailed evaluations and documentation of emergency changes should be completed as soon as possible after changes are implemented. Management should test routine and, whenever possible, emergency changes prior to implementation and quickly notify affected parties of all changes. If management is unable to thoroughly test emergency modifications before installation, it is critical that they appropriately backup files and programs and have established back-out procedures in place.

Software patches are similar in complexity to routine modifications. This document uses the term "patch" to describe program modifications involving externally developed software packages. However, organizations with in-house programming may also refer to routine software modifications as patches. Patch management programs should address procedures for evaluating, approving, testing, installing, and documenting software modifications. However, a critical part of the patch management process involves maintaining an awareness of external vulnerabilities and available patches.

Maintaining accurate, up-to-date hardware and software inventories is a critical part of all change management processes. Management should carefully document all modifications to ensure accurate system inventories. (If material software patches are identified but not implemented, management should document the reason why the patch was not installed.)

Management should coordinate all technology related changes through an oversight committee and assign an appropriate party responsibility for administering software patch management programs. Quality assurance, security, audit, regulatory compliance, network, and end-user personnel should be appropriately included in change management processes. Risk and security review should be done whenever a system modification is implemented to ensure controls remain in place.

Disposal Phase

The disposal phase involves the orderly removal of surplus or obsolete hardware, software, or data. Primary tasks include the transfer, archiving, or destruction of data records. Management should transfer data from production systems in a planned and controlled manner that includes appropriate backup and testing procedures. Organizations should maintain archived data in accordance with applicable record retention requirements. It should also archive system documentation in case it becomes necessary to reinstall a system into production. Management should destroy data by overwriting old information or demagnetizing disks and tapes.

Introduction Software System Analysis and Design (SSAD)

To solve a problem systems are created. One can think that a system approach is a way to solve a problem. In today's world, the subject system analysis and design, manly work with software development activities.

Objectives

In this unit we are going to understand.

- a system
- the different phases of system developments life cycle
- the components of system analysis
- the components of system designing

Defining a System

A group of components that work together to achieve an objective is called a system. In every system there are three components namely input, processing & output.

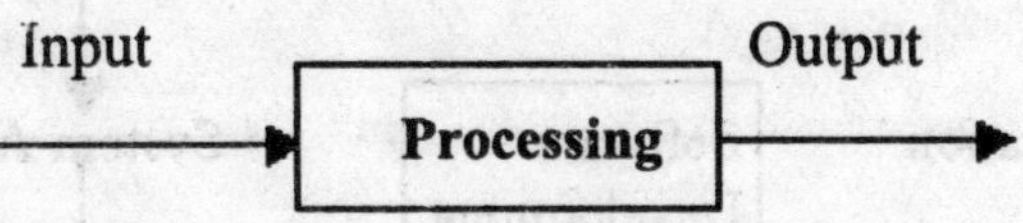

In a system all these different component are interdependent on each other. For example, Human body is considered to be complete natural system. We are also surrounded by many environmental system such as political system, economic system, educational system and so forth. The objective of the system is that after processing of desired input output is produced.

System Life Cycle

System life cycle is used for developing and maintaining system. It helps in developing a system project plan; it is necessary for building a system. Meaning of system development life cycle is the combination of various activities. In other words we can say that various activities are put together are referred to as system development life cycle.

In the system analysis and design terminology, the system development life cycle means software development life cycle. Software development cycle have following different phases.

Following are the different phases of software development cycle:

- System study
- Feasibility study
- System analysis
- System design
- Coding
- Testing
- Implementation
- Maintenance

The different phases of software development life cycle is shown in Figure

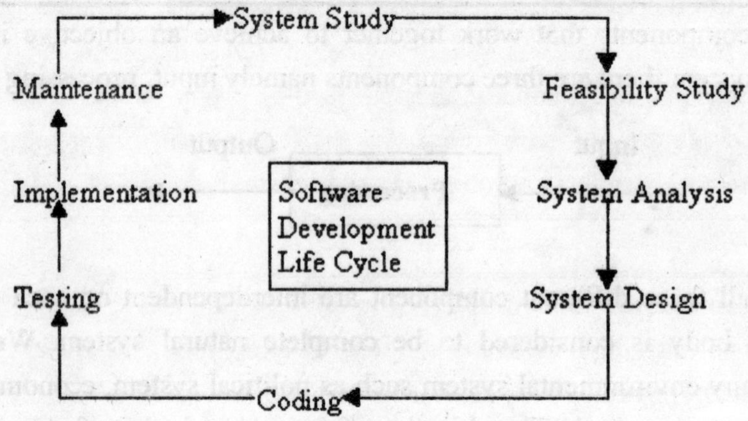

Fig. Different phases of Software development Life Cycle

Phases of System Development Life Cycle

Description of different phases & related activities of system development life cycle are:-

System Study

The initial stage of system development life cycle is system study. This shares a clear picture of what exactly the physical system is. In practical, through true phases system study can be done.

In first phase with the help of identification of scope of the system the preliminary survey of the system can be done.

In the second phase of the system study is more detailed and in depth study in which the present system is studied.

After completing system study, system analyst prepares a system proposal and passes in to the user. The proposed system contain the finding of the present system and recommendation to overcome the limitations and problems of the present system in the light of the user's requirement.

To study deeply about system study phase following has to be done

- problem identification and project initiation
- background analysis
- inference or findings

Feasibility Study

Feasibility study take place on the basis of consequence of initial study with the help of feasibility study we can make the test of proposed system in the light of its work ability meeting user's requirements, effective use of resource an course, the cost effectiveness. The main aim of feasibility study is to achieve scope and not to solve the problem. In feasibility study, cost & benefits are estimated with great accuracy.

System Analysis

Assuming that a new system is to be developed, the next phase is system analysis. In analysis we study the details of operation to carry out. and their connection with and outside the system. During analysis data are assembled in a file which can be used during decision making. For system analysis we use interviews, on site observation and questionnaire. To draw the exact boundary of the new system under consideration we follow the under mentioned steps:-

- Keeping in view the problems and new requirements
- Workout the pros and cons including new areas of the system

Through the use of DFD (Data Flow Diagrams) all procedure necessities must be recognize and documented. Sub-dividing of complex process involving the entire system, identification of data store and manual processes are included in system analysis. System analysis includes following main points.

- Specification of what the new system is to accomplish based on the user requirements.
- Functional hierarchy showing the functions to be performed by the new system and their relationship with each other.
- Function network which are similar to function hierarchy but they highlight the those functions which are common to more than one procedure.
- List of attributes of the entities - these are the data items which need to be held about each entity (record)

System Design

Based on user requirements and detailed analysis of a new system, the new system must be designed. This is the phase of system designing. It is the most important phase in development of a system. Following are the two stages on which the design proceed.

- preliminary or general design
- Structure or detailed design

Preliminary or general design: The features of the new system are specified in the preliminary or general design. The cost involved in this feature and benefits derived are taken. More of this process is done in the design stage, if the project is considered as feasible.

Structure or Detailed design: In the detailed design stage, computer oriented work begins in earnest. At this stage the design of the system becomes more structured. Structure design is a blue print of computer system solution to a given problem housing the same components & interrelationship among the same components and the original problem. Input, output and processing specifications are drawn up in detail. In the design stage the programming language & the platform in which the new system will run are also decided.

There are following tools and technique use for designing.

- Data flow diagram (DFDs)
- Data dictionary
- Structured English
- Decision table
- Decision tree

Above mention tools are design are discussed in the next lesson.

Coding

After the new system is designed, the whole system is required to be transform into computer language which a computer can understand. Computer programming language does coding in the new system. It is most crucial stage, in which with the support of computer language the defined procedure are converted into control specification. This is also known as programming phase in which programmer transform the program specification into computer instruction which came to be known as programs. The programs coordinate the data movements and control the entire process in a system. It is generally left that programs are standardize in nature. Fast development, maintenance & future change help by this, needed.

Testing

Before actually implementing the new system into operations, a test run of the system is done removing all the bugs, if any. In successful system this a most important phase. When the whole program of the system is coded, a test plan is built and run on given set of test data. The expected result must match to the output of the list run.

By utilizing the last data following list run are carried out:

- Unit test
- System test

Unit Test

There will be individually listed with the prepared test data, when the program is coded & computed and brought all together in working condition, Any error must be debugged.

System Test

After carrying out the unit test for each of the programs of the system and when errors are removed, the system test is considered as complete. On the actual data the whole system is processed. The consequences or output of the system is analyzed at each stage of execution, During the result analysis, it may be found that the output is mismatching the expected system. In this case in a particular program error are found out and are fixed & further tested for output which is expected, when it is confirmed that the system is running free error, the users are asked to use the actual data so that the system could be shown running as per their need.

Implementation

Implementation phase starts after having user acceptance of the new system built. All programs are loaded in the users computer during this phase. Training starts as soon as the user system is loaded with the newly made package. Main topic of such type of training are :

- How to execute the package
- How to enter the data
- How to process the data (processing details)
- How to take out the reports

Manual working is transferred to computerized working when the users are trained about the new system. For running the system the following two strategies are followed :

(i) **Parallel run:** In this both computerized & manual system are run in parallel for a certain defined period. This is done because:-

- Comparisons are made between manual result and computerized results.
- There is no effect on the working of organization even if the computerized system fails at the early stage, because system continue to work, as it used to do.

(ii) **Pilot run:** The system are installed in parts in this process. In the beginning some parts of new system is installed, when it runs successfully for a notable time period then other parts are implemented. This strategy builds the confidence and errors are traced easy

Maintenance

To avoid errors while a system is working, timely maintenance is required. For this it requires review of the system from time to time. Review of the system can be done for

- knowing the full capabilities of the system
- knowing the required changes or the additional requirements
- studying the performance

If a major change is needed, a new project may have to be set up to carryout the change. The new project will then proceed through all the above life cycle phases.

Object-oriented Architecture

Everything (processes, files, I/O operation, etc.) is represented as a object in this architecture. Objects are data structure in memory that may be handled by whole system (hardware and software), For the high level user interface they give high level description. Names, and labels are descriptors in objects. Information like type of object and a description capabilities that apply to a particular object are given by descriptors. Object oriented architecture system can also be known as extension or generalization of capability architecture system, and contain same capability to provide basis for protection and computer security.

Encapsulation, Polymorphism and inheritance are essentials in object oriented systems.

It's also possible to do without them (e.g., in visual basic applications and visual basic) and yet program with constructs that models real world entitles.

Class

Abstract characteristics of a thing are defined, involving thing's characteristics, its attributes, fields or properties and the behaviors (what it can do or methods, operations or features) It can be stated that class is a blue print or factory that describes the nature of something for instance a German shepherd dog has trait shared by all dogs, such as breed & fur colors (characteristic), the ability to bark & sit. Modularity is given by class and structure is a project oriented computer program. A class should typically be re-organzable.. Members are the properties & methods define by class.

REVIEW QUESTIONS

1. Define a system. Explain the components of a system.
2. What do you understand by system development life cycle?
3. Discuss the importance of system analysis and design in the development of a system?
4. Define Object oriented architecture.
5. What do you understand by inheritance?
6. What do you understand by polymorphism?
7. What do you understand by Encapsulation?
8. What do you understand class?
9. What do you understand object?
10. What do you understand method?
11. What do you understand message passing?

6 ERP Implementation Strategy

Introduction

Various companies are in the trend of implementing ERP to their organization for streamline the work process and increase efficiency in working and increase the effectiveness of the employees.

For this there are several implementation processes which are the variants of the under mentioned basic types. The success and failure of ERP in an organization depends upon the implementation process.

(1) Big Bang

(2) Phased

(3) Parallel

(4) Process line

(5) Hybrid

This technique concentrate on the plan of how to make transition from legacy system to a new ERP system.

The three pillar that help any ERP implementation i.e.

(*i*) Process

(*ii*) People

(*iii*) Technology

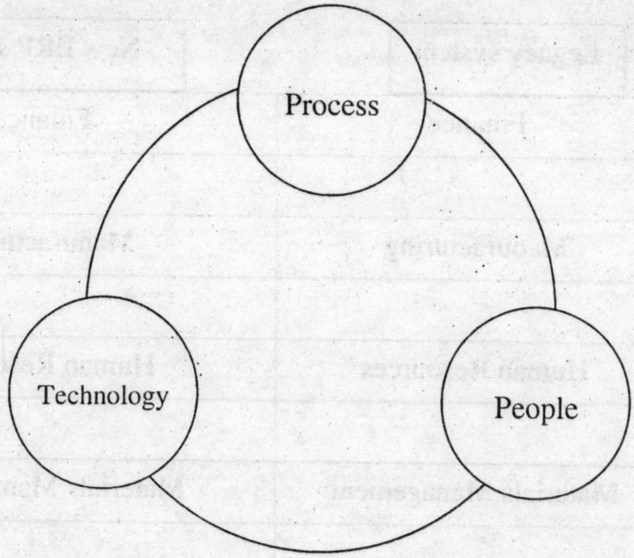

Big Bang Strategy

This strategy is opposite to phased, module by module shift to the new system from the old one. The shift is made on a scheduled date for the entire organization in a single instance.

This involves a need of huge training to the users of the previous system. In this process a lot of customization is also needed. The aim of this process is to reduce cost and increase productivity.

The following advantages is offers by big bang if it is utilize properly.

1. It ignores complex integration issues.
2. It gives strong control focus for all ERP team member.
3. The overall cost of implementation is low because no interface programs are required for communicating between the legacy system to new ERP system

Some of the disadvantages that big ban strategy include.

1. The extent of time, cautious planning & preparation for going live is more.
2. Bottleneck of critical resources, like shortage of fund and non-availability of professional etc. during the implementation can result in failed implementation.

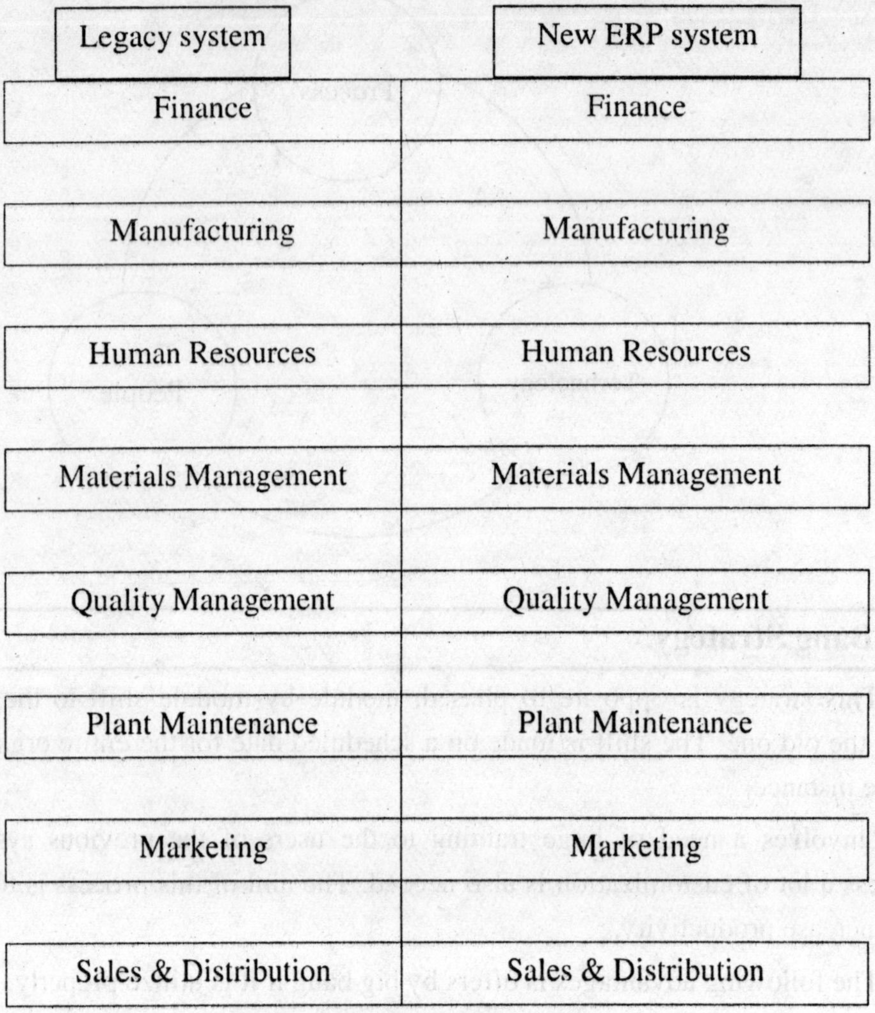

Fig. (a) Big Bang Transition

Big Bang Variants

Various variants of Big Bang strategy are :

1. Mini big bang
2. Mega big bang
3. Multi big bang

Phased Implementation

Phased approach, implements one functional module at a time, in sequence order. Modular, functional or sequential implementation are the names that are given to this approach. This approach suits companies that do not share many common process across department or business units.

For the phased approach interface progress are ordinary, or various situation consist of phasing, there is need of interface to bridge the space between legacy system and new ERP system, until the new ERP system becomes fully functional.

This is a close relationship between phased approach & big bang approach.

Advantages of this approach are :

1. One functional module at a time is implementation before another is attempted.
2. By taking this stabbing stone approach many companies feel more comfortable.
3. More flexibility may also be gained.

Disadvantages of this approaches

1. Cost and time to implement is much higher by using this approach
2. There is an expectation among key ERP team member because of time taking duration that usually accompany this approach.

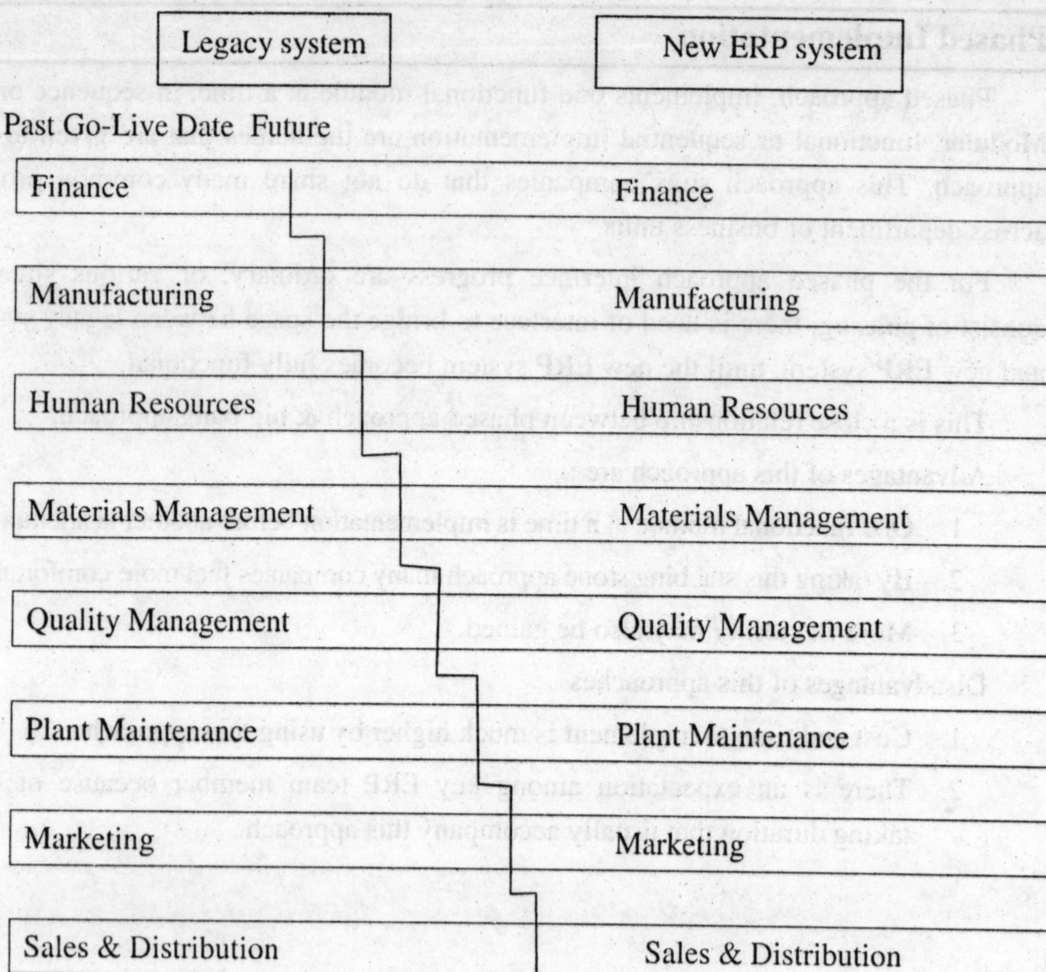

Fig. (b) Phased ERP Implementation

Parallel Implementation

Parallel approach activates both new ERP system and legacy system for a length of time.

Both the systems are in the operation from one day to several months. Finance, manufacturing, marketing are the portion of similar functional business area which work at same time for legacy & ERP system.

There is an option of recovery in parallel approach which is used when something goes wrong. This is the advantage of parallel approach.

In real world condition on exact number comparison is given in parallel approach. In parallel approach resources are consumed in much higher amount than using other techniques. Confusion arises when both systems are not interacting.

The parallel approach is ideally suited for mission critical situation that cannot survive a major malfunction of an ERP system

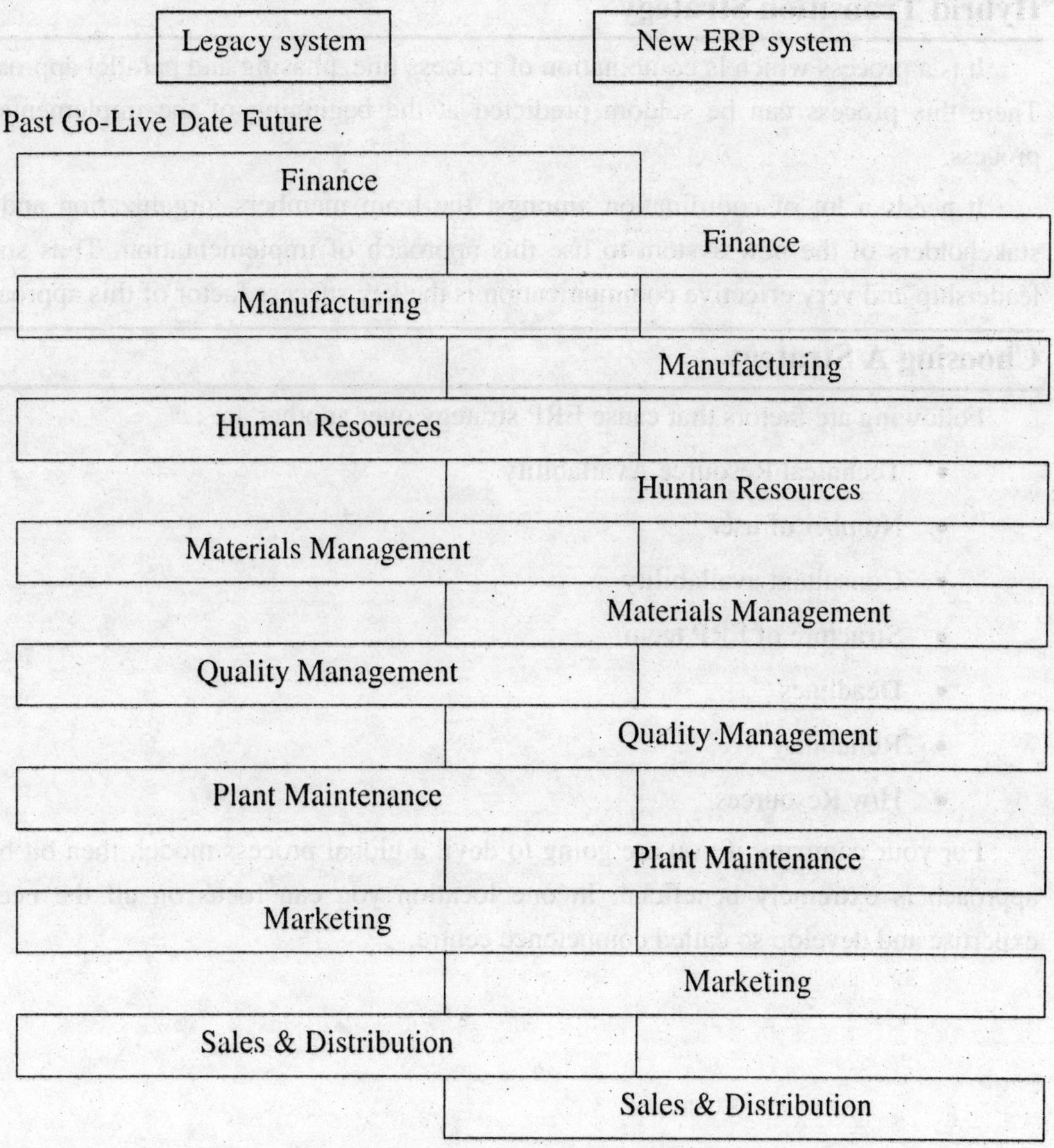

Fig. (c) ERP Transition Strategy

Process Line Transition Strategy

The process of line strategy and mini big bang are both similar conceptually. For the management of parallel business process favors product line, the implementation strategy is broken by process line strategy.

Hybrid Transition Strategy

It is a process which is combination of process line, phasing and parallel approach.. There this process can be seldom predicted at the beginning of the implementation process.

It needs a lot of coordination amongst the team members, organization and the stakeholders of the new system to use this approach of implementation. Thus strong leadership and very effective communication is the key success factor of this approach.

Choosing A Strategy

Following are factors that cause ERP strategy over another are :

- Technical Resource Availability
- Number of user
- Consultant availability
- Structure of ERP teem
- Deadlines
- Reliability
- H/w Resources

For your company if you are going to devil a global process model, then bit bong approach is extremely beneficial. In one location you can focus on all the needed expertise and develop so called competence centre.

REVIEW QUESTIONS

(1) Explain the big bang strategy with the help of a diagram.

(2) Explain the phased ERP implementation strategy with the help of a diagram.

(3) Explain the parallel ERP implementation strategy with the help of a diagram.

(4) Explain the process-line transition strategy with the help of a diagram.

(5) Explain the hybrid transition strategy.

(6) How do you choose a transition strategy?

(7) What are interface programs and why are they used in the phased approach?

(8) What are the transition strategies or methodologies for implementing ERP systems?

7 VENDORS, CONSULTANTS AND EMPLOYEES

In-house ERP Development

To develop an ERP package is a tough task to be done, because it involves cost, time, a huge manpower and other resources of the organization. Companies have skilled professionals in their ITES departments. There skilled professional have much experience in building complex system but building of such high developed & complex system like ERP may vary in terms of competency of these companies. It is a better proposition for these companies to utilize their resources to make their products and services better so that they can serve better to their customers rather concentrating on developing such a huge software package.

It is not possible for the companies mostly to compare the quality, scope, functionality or technology of the systems created by those, whose main business is to develop software.

Thus developing an in house ERP is not a good business proposition..

In-House ERP Implementation

It is not a easy task to implement an ERP system successfully. It involve huge investment, so it cannot be done on trial basis.

Many ERP vendors have their own team of consultants who suggest that the package is implemented following standard methodology. Different skill and approaches are needed for the development of ERP package and for implementing it. Vendors, consultants, in house team and end users are various groups of people involved in implementation and each has their own role to play.

Following are the knowledge and skill which in house personnel identified to do the job which help them to implement successfully within a reasonable time frame.

In house implementation have following constraint:

- With minimum manpower it is difficult to take responsibility of improving are competencies.
- Even after implementation, experts are hired and put them on company's' rolls.
- After implementation there is no need to waste a resources and spend a lot on training.
- Familiarity with ERP package and technical issues
- Spent at least one year on ERP systems with hands on experience.
- Knowledge of how to organize and run a project of such magnitude
- Experience in handling problems and issues during implementation
- Good Man management skills
- Good leadership skills
- Excellent training skills

Constraints in In-House implementations are:

- Difficulty in taking the total responsibility of improving core competencies with reduced manpower
- Hiring experts and keeping them on company's pay rolls even after implementation
- Wasting a lot of resources and spending a lot on training most of which may not be needed after implementation

Cost-Benefit Analysis

Various alternatives assess effectively in this method. Each alternative has cost and benefit associated with it, which are compared with that of other alternative so that best alternative can be achieved. Cost benefit analysis provides costs, benefit and rule associated with each alternative:

- Identification of the costs and benefits related to the alternative
- Categorizing various costs and benefits
- Selecting a method of evaluation

- Interpreting the results of analysis and taking actions

All type of costs can be classified as tangible or intangible, direct or indirect, fixed and variable.

Cost Analysis

Here the cost analysis is done by various cost elements of the system. Various cost elements are :

- Hardware Cost
- Personnel Cost
- Facility Cost
- Operating Cost
- Supply Cost
- Maintenance Cost

Benefit Analysis

It is expected from every alternative that it provide certain benefits. In this analysis, every benefit is analyze & assigned a monetary value to at Benefit are classified as tangible or intangible, direct or indirect, fixed & variable, like cost.

Various types of cost & tangible benefits are:

- **Tangible Costs & Tangible Benefits are :** These are measurable. Tangible cost like hardware, software training cost or salaries tangible benefit is finishing job in limited hours.
- **Intangible Costs & Intangible Benefits:** These are not measurable. Implementation effect on goodwill of the company is intangible cost. Intangible cost is customer satisfaction.
- **Direct Costs & Direct Benefits:** Monetary values are associated with this. Direct cost is stationary cost. In direct benefits system handle more work.
- **Indirect Costs & Direct Benefits:** includes overheads and the benefits derived from them
- **Fixed Costs & Fixed Benefits:** These are set and can be change at all.

- **Variable Costs & Variable Benefits:** There are volume oriented costs & change with volume of work.

After the identification of cost and benefits, analysis is done by utilizing any of the following technique.

- Net Benefit Analysis
- Present Value Analysis
- Net Present Value Analysis
- Payback Analysis
- Break Even Analysis
- Cash Flow Analysis

Detailed Analysis

Detailed Analysis helps to give solution to the problem in term of specification to meet user requirement in this phase following task are included :

- Examine & document the features, shortcoming and problems of existing system.
- Analyze the findings and record the results
- Define and document the proposed system
- Verify the proposed system
- Generate a detailed report supporting the proposal
- Estimate resources needed to design and implement the proposed system.

Design

This phase is very creative and crucial. Entire proposed system is defined and constructed during this phase. Task include :

- Appraising of terms of reference or scope of work
- Appraising the problem areas of existing system
- Defining the goal of proposed ERP system
- Determine the input requirements to achieve the defined goal
- Deciding platform and file system

- Deciding on programming language and data structure
- Designing the output forms
- Documenting all aspects of design in detail

Implementation

In this phase the design is put to work and main task is to make the system operational. Tasks involve the following.

- Selection and preparation of site
- Hardware and software are in place
- Loading of application software
- Configuration
- Testing
- User training
- Providing Security to System
- Assigning Access privilege to users

Post Implementation

In this phase, all the support services are provided to keep the system operational. Following maintenance are carried out:

- Corrective Maintenance: Fixing bugs, repairing processing failures
- Adaptive Maintenance: Changing program function
- Perceptive Maintenance: Change requirements to meet user's need

Vendors

ERP packages are developed by the vendors and these packages are supplied by them by investing huge amount of money, time and efforts in research and engineering of these packaged solution. Every ERP package is developed from the observation of a group of people working in a specific business that develop system to handle certain business segment.

Aim of the vendors entering the ERP market is to have competitive edge. There are features and functionality in the ERP packages to meet the business needs of almost all the sectors. Hence, to keep face with new & latest technologies vendors are required to upgrade their package.

Role of the Vendor:

Once it is in place, ERP systems are used by people who are the employees. Role of employees is most critical, as they play operational roles and measure the success after ERP has been implemented. There are changes in the post implementation, employee job profiles and responsibility. Employee will be given training to use the new system. Though they could have initial apprehension about new system replacing the existing jobs, amount of training they have to undergo, taking up new responsibility but all these fears can be removed from employee's mind by addressing to their various fears and problems. Fact, they should be firmly persuaded as how new system support them to remove monotonous clerical work and transmit themselves into highly valued individual challenging work environment. ERP implementation does not provide desired results even though the support & cooperation are given by the employees.

Role of vendor

- Supply the product along with documentation
- Fix any problem in the software encountered during implementation
- Provide initial training for the company's key personnel playing lead role during implementation
- Provide project support and quality control
- Advise implementation team on finer aspects leading to performance improvement.
- Modify the product in case customization is required to suit company's need.
- Make regular upgrades available to company.

Consultants

- Consultants are professionals who have skills in establishing technology & methodologies working with ERP implementation. They are masters in implementation life cycle and have many years of experience gained by personal observation or contact with various industries.
- According to statistics, a successfully implemented ERP system pays back over a period of 10 & 20 months. It is indicated by cost break up that the fee of

consultant is about 1.5 to 2 time the cost of software product. Despite all this money spent on good consultation is still worth the investment as expertise of the consultations is in available that will ensure successful implementation. To find the consultants with necessary know how who will the most important thing.

- A consultant should work with company personnel.
- They should transfer the knowledge to the company's employees and make their services available in case of need

Role of the Consultant:

- The success of the project is warranted.
- Show the result of satisfaction of the company management.
- Activities are scheduled on scheduled time along with effective participation.
- For every phase times schedule is determine and project plan is finalize
- Use the correct methodology to do it right the first time leading to huge servings in money time & effect.
- Company's business processes are make better to map functionalities of product as much as possible.
- Balance loyalty between customer and vendor so as to benefit both.
- Alert the company management about the actions and decision required to be taken to ensure smooth progress of implementation.
- Technical documentation are maintained which are related to project.
- For building a knowledge base company's people are trained.

Employees

Employees are the people who will be using the ERP system once it is in place. Employees play most important role towards success of ERP implementation as they play operational roles and are means to measure the success after ERP is in place. Employees job profiles as well as responsibility will change in Post implementation. Employees will be given training to use the new system. Though, they would have initial apprehension about new system replacing their existing jobs, amount of training they have to undergo, taking up new responsibility but all these fears can be alleviated from employees mind by addressing them well in advance. In fact, they should be convinced as to how the new system can help them eliminating monotonous clerical work and transform themselves into highly valued individual in a new and challenging work environment using modern technology. With the support and cooperation from Employees, it is unlikely that ERP implementation will not bring the desired result.

REVIEW QUESTIONS

1. What are the services provided by the consultants?
2. What are the advantages and disadvantages of the in house ERP implementation?
3. Who are ERP package vendors?
4. What are the soles and responsibilities of the ERP vendors?
5. Explain the vendor management process.
6. Explain the role, duties and responsibilities of the consultants.
7. What are the main points that the contract with the vendor should address in addition to issues about source code and modifications?
8. What additional things should be included in the contract to safeguard the interests of the organization?
9. List some of the points that should be part of the contract with the consultants.

8 ERP vs. E-Commerce

1. Meaning of E-Commerce

The process of doing business by exchange of goods and services using internet as a medium is called e-commerce. It also includes activities which are important in a business such as advertising, marketing, customer support, delivery and payments.

There are various models of E-commerce.

- B2C E-Commerce
- B2B E-Commerce
- C2C E-Commerce

B2C E-Commerce is transaction between companies and customers. Reasons for using e-commerce to sell company's products are:

(*a*) Good way to reach customer leading to improved sales

(*b*) Improve customer specific marketing using Data Mining thereby increasing sales & profit

(*c*) Improve efficiency by streamlining operations and increasing profit.

(d) Provide convenience to the customers

ERP and E-Commerce both are complimentary to each other, where ERP is the backend application and E-Commerce is frontend application. Both works simultaneously to support each other. Company using E-commerce to do business will not survive well if it is not backed up with ERP, as ERP enables speedy web orders fulfillment, customer support and many such tasks which are very critical in success of a business.

A company website receiving any order, first has to be directed to the respective department like marketing, manufacturing, shipping and accounting which is also called back office processing. The back office operation is critical for any company's success.

One major cause in the failure of fulfilling website orders in time is due to un-integrated back office system, where there is no information sharing between warehouse and order fulfillment system. For example a toy company should have sufficient toys to fulfill all orders but it is not possible for a company to organize most basic functions like picking, packing and shipping to deliver if one of the components is not complying to the supply chain process. Thus, integration of Internet front office operation and ERP back office operation is must is today's business environment.

2. Future Directives in ERP

In present scenario of new innovations, ERP being a prevailing technology gives a tough competition to new cutting age technologies like E-Commerce and EDI and competitive new business practices involving SCM and CRM.

2.1 New Markets and New Channels

Due to rapid implementation of ERP solution in large and developing enterprises, market vendors are forced to shift their interest towards new markets to restrain their growth. Following are the initiatives taken by vendors to increase their appeal to small business clients:

- Supplementing direct sales force with reseller channels
- Lowering price of software to make it more viable
- Increase appeal on basis of reduced functionality
- Using better implementation methodologies for faster deployment
- Inter-portability of products between various platforms

Vendors have taken up new markets and new channels to reach smaller business which are looking for one stop shopping for their solutions.

Vendor moving in this direction are Oracle and JD Edwards. Oracle made entry in the middle level market while JD Edwards complemented with its one world suit with a lower cost product called Genesis, other vendors are yet to take initiative to come out with light version product to suit middle market.

2.2 Faster Implementation Methodologies

As of to-day ERP implementation remains a difficult proposition due to:

- Complexities in the software
- High cost of software
- High cost of implementation
- Long time for implementation

Cost and time are interrelated to each other by vendors for implementation. They are interrelated as longer the implementation time, higher the cost. Few vendors believe in reducing the implementation time so as to cut down cost by:

- Providing more effective tools to accelerate the process
- Creating elite consulting team to back up resources when required
- Using modular approach to facilitate easier integration.

Hence, to provide faster implementation:

A tool launched by SAP is ASAP (accelerated SAP). Implementation time can be reduced to a great extent (less than 6 months) if the lessons are taken from implementation of R/3 where the implementations are done by configuring one module at a time and then following the steps for further process.

Oracle introduced a program called past forward to speed up implementation.

To carry on the implementation several vendors have created highly skilled consultant teams with fully trained and experienced consultants among which Oracles oracle one & SAP's platinum are few consulting services.

2.3 APIs

Demands for open markets will increasing rapidly in future due to increasing demands from clients to integrate various technologies.

SAP has launched specification for (70 business FPIS helping third party applications interact with R/3 directly. BAPI(Business Application Programming Interface) are set of methods which allows external application to interact though specific R/3 objects such as customer accounts or employees.

Baan provides org-ware, that utilizes tightly integrated business modeling tool which will helps automatic configuration to suit specific needs. Company is presently enhancing this particular category of tool to accelerate implementation on window NT platform.

2.4 Inter-operability of Platforms

Due to rising popularity of window NT, the ERP vendors delivery their product compatible with NT platform

- SAP R/3 is available on NT since 1994 and on SQL Server since 1995.
- Baan, Oracle and PeopleSoft have come with their version in 1997.
- SAP has over 2000 R/3 installations on NT. Baan sports the *'Designated for Microsoft BackOffice '* certification. Oracle has its support for its own NT-based clustering technology and PeopleSoft has recently shifted to BackOffice as primary development and initial rollout platform.

Middle mark vendors are opting for back office platform with preferred combination of NT SOL server.

2.5 New Business Segments

Few vendors are capable of serving vertical markets such as Government healthcare, financial services or Retail distribution. While some other vendors are capable in serving areas as SCM and demand forecasting or sales automation and marketing.

Red Pepper software is opted by people soft to enhance its supply chain while BAAR AURUN software is opted by Baan to enhance its CRM tool and it also collaborate with Hyperion software to strengthen its finance module by connecting its distribution and manufacturing modules to Hyperons Financial Accounting, Budgeting and Reporting solution.

DSS has been another future area where all the ERP vendors are focusing. BaaN is linking its applications to Gentia product to provide ***OLAP*** capabilities.

JD Edwards teamed with Information Builders to deliver a ***Data Mart***

Oracle provides a *Data Mart* designer and builder tool for creating data marts. It also offers Oracle Discoverer, a tool for querying, charting and reporting.

PoepleSoft would integrate its application with Powerplay multidimensional *OLAP* tool from Cognos Corp and Arbor Software Corp's multidimensional escape server.

SAP has synchronized R/3 system with *Data Warehouse* that can manage both R/3 and non-R/3 data through use of a metadata repository and a front-end OLAP engine.

2.6 Impact of Internet on ERP Products

Through the emergence of internet and www an ERP product will be impacted along with other software product vendors of ERP are compell to more from client server to browser/server architecture to web enable their product so as to hand over. Self service & e-commerce ability or power.

Baan in all its products uses Java based web interface. It also concentration:

Baan is using Java based Web interface to all its products. It also focusing on

- Automation of supply chain relationship via Internet
- E-Commerce via Site Server
- Report and Alert distribution across Web using Hyperion Software Corp.'s Spider-Man technology

People soft is set to deliver its universal applications Java based self services appeals with its people soft-7.

JD Edwards is utilizing Java to pursuit its one world functionality to be obtainable either through a window client or web browser. Java is utilized by Oracle to deliver its Oracle Web Customers & Oracle Web Supplier modules.

25 web applications were released by SAP for version JI of R/3.

For the first generation of web enabled products ERP vendor are utilizing Java. Move by ERP vendors to embrace JAVA to deliver & deploy web functionality is first more preferring use of open tools compared to proprietary technologies.

2.7 Future Market

ERP market - Just this minute - First published 2003, still valid

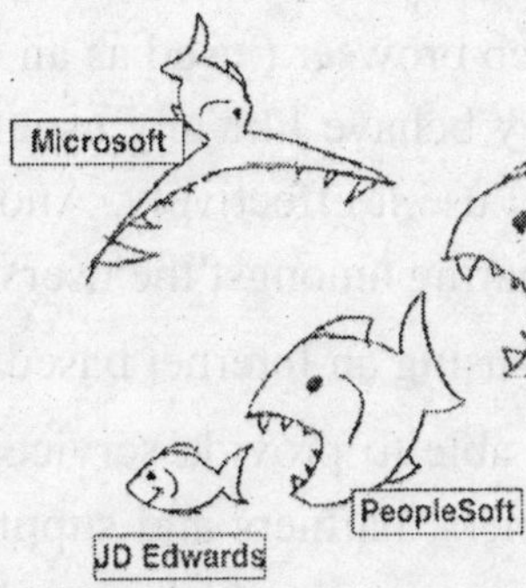

Source: www.dpu.se (Data Research DPU)

ERP market has evolved from the 1980s till date. Enterprise Resource Planning solutions are now a days not only built for large fortune 500 companies but currently all companies be it large, medium or small are adopting ERP solution suited for their business needs. ERP solutions been seen in two and three tier form, as SaaS (Software as a Service) solutions, and even as open source solutions.

Where does the future of ERP hold when there are so many ways to deliver an ERP solution to the companies? The answer to this question is that more small businesses are implementing ERP solutions, which means that there's tons of money to be made in the small business ERP market.

Some vendors in the global ERP market are; SAP, Oracle. QAD, Ramco, CDC Software, COA Solutions, Consona Corporation, Unit 4 Agresso NV, Plex Systems, Epicor, and ABAS Software. Thus it is becoming obvious that the future of ERP is getting to be very strong. With the evolution of the internet, SaaS and open source ERP products will also flourish.

3. ERP and Internet

Till now we have learned that a client/server-based architecture very complicated and expensive be implemented in an enterprise. The time and resources taken for implementation (for 18 month-2 year), followed by constant desktop training and support makes it too expensive and to top of it, if there is a flaw in implementation process then there is every chance that the ERP will fail. Thus is was felt that there is a need for cost-effective enterprise solutions that can be easily implemented and readily accessed across the enterprise.

An Internet-based enterprise software system lessens the training and maintenance costs as in those systems a standard Web browser (used as an user interface) is used to operate these complex systems but they behave like any usual Web-based application, making it easier for people to learn and use it effectively. Another benefit using such a system is that it helps in information sharing amongst the users.

Following are the major benefits of using an Internet based ERP system:

1. Ubiquity : Company should be able to provide services and business processes both to current and prospective customers, partners and suppliers. For this the current available system as well as the new system should be available to the users of the organization. Nowadays no organization can afford not to reach a global audience by creating an operational or support issue for those to be reached . Thus Internet based enterprise applications can be easily extended to employees, partners, suppliers and customers regardless of geographies and languages.

2. Usability: Almost everyone in an organization uses a Web browser. Thus by making enterprise applications available in this format, an organization has two benefits:

a. lower training costs (which lower the software's total cost of ownership),
b. increased user acceptance (which greatly improves the project's chances of success).

To maximize use and minimize training costs, the enterprise applications should be available in a consistent fashion to everyone wherever they are. By improving upon the reachability, navigability, independent of the users location, the acceptance from and success increases.

3. Integration: Integration costs is almost 40 per cent of the average installation cost. Using an Internet based architecture can help to reduce the costs of integration. The architecture integrates the system using technologies like HTTP and XML, and support standards such as J2EE and standard application servers such as WebSphere and WebLogic to maximize the potential collaboration between the new and existing corporate systems.

For example : J.D. Edwards also spent the late 1990s and early 2000s retooling itself. The firm made its first acquisition in 1999, paying $12 million for The Premisys Corp., a sales automation software provider. The firm also purchased supply chain software provider Numetrix, eventually adding supply chain functionality to its OneWorld suite. J.D. Edwards also pursued deals with Siebel Systems Inc. for access to its CRM applications and with Ariba Inc. for B2B e-commerce technology. Although the alliance with Siebel Systems eventually proved fairly fruitless, the firm did eventually acquire CRM technology via its September 2001 purchase of Youcentric Inc. Late in 2000, the firm unveiled OneWorld Xe, which used the Web's extended markup language (XML) technology to allow clients to electronically connect to business partners using other platforms and software applications (*citation 53*)

4. Becoming A Real-time Enterprise: Real-time enterprise is an organization that has moved its business processes to Internet and is connected will the people that touch its business directly to these processes in real-time.

This helps businesses in several ways:

a. It lets the organization constantly monitor the business processes (sales cycle, supply chain, financial operations, staffing, etc.

b. It gives access to information at the point of customer interaction.

c. It helps to react (take decision) instantly to business changes.

The benefits of an Internet enterprise software implementation extends well beyond cost-effective deployment and maintenance. It is the only way of creating a real-time enterprise, which helps in increasing revenues, reducing costs and enhancing profitability.

4. Critical Success Factors

Huge investment and complexities are involve in ERP. Results of an ERP implementation in an organization can be destructive; sometimes organization is excluded from business. Following factors have been identified as critical foe h success of an ERP implementation.

- **Strong Executive Level Commitment**

Large investment needed to implement ERP must ensure that decisions are invariably taken at executive level, which amounts to involvement but not commitment. But it is also imperative that top management remains committed during the implementation process like involving best people in the project, resisting over customization

- **Change Management**

ERP implementation brings in large-scale change in role and working culture Unless top management is involved directly, it is impossible for any line manager to face the opposition to change

- Project Management
- Adequate Training
- Communication
- Clear Project Vision
- Business Process Change
- Hiring Consultants
- Business case
- Adequate testing
- Adequate software selection
- When selecting an ERP following points need to be taken into consideration:
- Functional fit with business processes
- Integration between various components of ERP system
- Flexibility
- Complexity
- Use friendliness
- Quick implementation
- Ability to support multi-site planning and control
- Technology
- Regular upgrades
- Amount of customization required
- Local support infrastructure

- Availability of reference sites
- Total cost
- Integration with other software
- Implementation Approach
- Benchmarking
- Legacy system evaluation
- Implementation Strategy

Thus it can be seen that Strong Executive Level Commitment is the most critical factor towards ensuring success of ERP implementation. Large investments involved in the implementation which makes it all the more important, that decisions are taken at top management or executive level.

Change Management is a very critical factor for success or failure of ERP implementation. ERP is likely to bring massive change in the organization. Unless top management is involved directly, it would be impossible for any line manager to face the opposition to such change.

It is quite surprising to note that Implementation Strategy is considered least critical for success though much of stress is given on working out a Strategy to ensure success.

Critical Failure Factors

Following have been identified as the critical factors which lead to the failure of an ERP project implementation to fail.

- In order of criticality, failure factors are:
- Lack of Executive Level Commitment
- Lack of focus on Change Management
- Poor Communication
- Lack of focus on Business Process Change
- Inadequate training
- Problems related to Project Management
- Change in Project Vision or Scope

- Inadequate Benchmarking
- Inadequate Legacy system evaluation
- No proper formulation of strategy
- Implementation Approach
- Inadequate testing
- Lack of support from consultant
- Inadequate software selection
- Not working on the business case
- Failure to integrate with other software

As can be seen, factors are same. Only lack and inadequacy of these factors can turn success into failure.

As ERP brings in massive transformation, many employees find it difficult to accept. If employees are not provided adequate training and education on ERP in advance, then the system will fail. Another factor is fear of unemployment/redundancy of job. When procedure becomes automated, people who were doing those jobs earlier become redundant. So it is quite natural to have resistance from employees. But same employees can be trained in the new system so that they accept the change as challenge and put in their best in new environment.

Without support from employees even the best system will fail. So it is very important that management take necessary steps to alleviate the fears and provide necessary training to its employees.

5. Integrating ERP into Organizational Culture

Integrated data model is the main part of any ERP system, from different locations employees are provided facilities of sharing resource for required data by accessing the remote files. For analysis and decision making data either kept centrally or they are kept in a distributed database. The basic advantage of distributed database is user mobility and response time. Centralized database, on other hand, offer ease of management and administration.

Integrated database are impressive and gives precise and reliable information to its users as all the data structure and processes are integrated by it so that real image of enterprise are reflected.

It offers data update in real time environment.

These integration features are attracting more companies to go for ERP solution as part of their business solution. Though large companies invest more on ERP packages, mid size companies look for following before investing:

- End Product Optimization
- Reduction in Cycle Time
- Timely Completion of Accounts
- Dissemination of timely & accurate information to sales & marketing system
- Areas of Integration
- Data Warehousing SCM
- Works Flow Management E-Commerce
- Documentation Management

ERP software is divided into different layers for different activities for saving customer cost with safe and reliable business.

Layer 1 Business Services

Layer 2 Customer Services

Layer 3 Consulting System Integration & Implementation

Layer 4 Infrastructure Services

Layer 5 Business Continuity

All above layers individually and collectively provide following managerial functions:

- Planning
- Inventory Management
- Materials Management
- Order Processing

- Manufacturing
- Purchasing
- Accounts & Finance
- Human Resource
- Finally, integration of these business areas facilitates:
- Cost & Cycle Time Reduction
- Business Practice Improvement
- Different Services/Product Offering
- Affordability in terms Module based implementation
- Global adaptability in terms of currencies
- Customized services
- Integrated Data Model

Integrated data model is backbone of any ERP system. It facilitates employees sharing resource from different locations and access remote files for required data. Integrated databases are effective and offer accurate and reliable information to its users as it integrates all the data structures and processes to reflect true image of the enterprise. Key features are:

- Provides always up-to-date information to all users
- Stores all transaction related details
- Provides detail as well as summarized information for top level managers
- Automatic real time update in system and transaction files
- Gives faster response to user queries.

SCM offers integration of different supply chain and facilities among all supply chain partners. Collectively, SCM & ERP provide intra and inter-organizational advantages to the enterprise. Integration of both is a complex task because of diverse platforms and would require transformation and migration of data into a pre-established standards.

There may be two types of linkages.

- ERP-ERP linkage: Different supply chain partners are directly linked and data flow is continuous and faster.
- ERP-SCM linkage: Middleware support is needed to act as an interface between two.

ERP & CRM Integration

CRM technology based companies are given primary importance. Integration of ERP with CRM helps in building the improved structure both in and outside the organization, CRM takes care of details about customer backed by internet, they form an extended enterprise.

ERP reaches customers and suppliers by way of using Internet based applications and CRM in conjunction with SCM provides improved functionality. Main advantage of ERP & CRM integration is that customers are able to interact with companies using channels like Telephone, Fax and other media elements and hence response to customer request would be a major challenge for the organization. CRM helps in addressing this and proved to be effective tool to manage customer details and respond to customer queries in effective manner. Internet provides a transparency between the systems. While customers can have access to data related to product price, its availability and order status etc., companies gather knowledge about customer and purchase pattern which can be used for marketing, Sales and production planning etc.

REVIEW QUESTIONS

1. Define ERP & E-Commerce.
2. Explain Future Directives- in ERP.
3. Clearly define ERP and Internet.
4. Define Critical success and failure factors.
5. Define Integrating ERP into organizational culture.

Case Study

Case Study of a Pharmaceutical Company Pliva

Since its 1996 listing on the London and Zagreb Stock Exchanges, PLIVA has made notable advancements in internationalizing its business and implementing global and innovative strategies. PLIVA is a rather unique company with investments in both research and development. With over 400 patents in its possession, PLIVA has proven the high calibre of its R&D capabilities, most notably through the discovery of its blockbuster - azithromycin. This macrolide antibiotic, globally known as Zithromax (under license to Pfizer) or Sumamed (PLIVA's brand), is the top selling antibiotic in its class.

PLIVA is the largest pharmaceutical company by turnover in Central and Eastern Europe and continues to expand its operations with recent acquisitions of pharmaceutical and R&D companies in the Czech Republic, France, Germany, United Kingdom and USA. With increasing efforts concentrating on the global pharmaceuticals market, PLIVA has divested its cosmetics, food and agrochemicals production units as standalone companies.

PLIVA consists of 44 legal entities, has 5 major business divisions (research, fine chemicals, pharmaceutical, OTC, DDI) and 9 strategic/corporate divisions (development, regulatory affairs, finance, human resources, IT, quality assurance, legal affairs, corporate communications and engineering). PLIVA employs almost 7500 people in 33 countries (including 120 IT professionals not including out -of-house consultants), has 5 main production locations (Croatia, Czech Republic, Poland, Germany and USA) and 43 subsidiaries in 23 countries.

SAP Software Solutions in PLIVA

The development of a modern ERP system to support these business operations, began in 1995/6 with projects intended to advance individual modules or sectors of IS. Up until that time, PLIVA had a classical transaction information system with centralized, hand-entered data. Pressured by a lack of time for independent development of a new integrated system, the management decided on the purchase of a complete system, keeping the SAP package in mind (alternatives were IBM, BAAN and Oracle). Today, according to the assessments of independent research, SAP Croatia holds 25% of the domestic business software market. In Croatia, SAP has 35 large clients including PLIVA, Podravka, Ericsson and Croatian Telecom, and most interestingly, the State Treasury (Vecernji List, 2002).

The implementation of the SAP solution took place in individual phases, with two modules in the area of cost center accounting and profit center accounting implemented in 1997. This enabled the better control of financial resources, forecasts and a new type of analysis.

During the implementation of the IS, the consulting company Price Waterhouse Coopers conducted a reengineering project, or the re-organization of business operations aimed at determining the key sectors of future operations: the 'core business'. Though these were two fully independent projects, they were harmonized at the level of the steering committee. SAP modules were implemented through 4 phases:

1. phase: 1996-1997 (SAP 3.0)

- FI-Financials
- CO-Controlling
- BC-Basis components
- UPGRADE 3.0-3.1 H
- **phase: 1998-2000**
- MM- Materials Management
- PP:-Production Planning
- QM-Quality Management
- SD-Sales & Distribution
- WM- Warehouse Management
- HR-Human Resources
- UPGRADE SAP 3.1H-4.0B-2000 (JAN)
- UPGRADE 4.0B-4.6 C 2000 (JULY)

3. phase: 2001

- PP-PI-Production Planning-Process industries-extension of PP module
- QM module-advanced functionality of Quality control

- PM-Plant Maintenance

4. phase: 2002

- International roll-out

A thorough review of the information system according to SAP specifications and standards was also conducted, and the implementation of the following modules is planned in 2003:

- SCM- Supply Chain Management,
- BIW- Business Information Warehouse,
- Project Systems, and
- Treasury

The transfer of operations to the new system (in the second phase of implementation) lasted 12 days, as the problem of shifting from the old coded system (taking over 'old' data) need to be resolved, and the process of preparations and system training lasted 4 months in 2 shifts, which included 700 employees (average training period of 7 days per employee). During the transfer to the new system, operations were halted for 10 days, while inventory and a detailed financial harmonization were conducted.

In addition to resistance to change (particularly emphasized with warehouse employees), the most significant problems in the system implementation were in the weak experience and quality of consultants who bid in the public tender, the lack of time and the specificity of the pharmaceutical industry (strictly regulated quality of raw materials, the obligation of non-stop production).

During the implementation of the new information system, and in running information systems in general, project organization with the usual participants stands out: the project sponsor, steering committee, project teams, team leader (most often a person outside the information specialization), functional teams and team members. An interesting organizational solution are the validation teams, which are separate from the project teams, and which have the task of control the teams' work, measuring harmonization with business plans and goals and coordinating the cross-functionality of teams. The validation team is led by a person from Quality Assurance), responsible for validating the information system, while the team members answer to the project manager for coordination and delivery, who is appointed by the director of QA (Quality Assurance). The members of the validation team are also team leaders for the remaining teams in the project. The Information Department in PLIVA has a strategic position in the company, is directly responsible to the company management and is developing as a profit center, meaning that daughter companies are billed for use of the information system and the transfer of the existing system is underway in the daughter companies (roll-out in 2003 in Czech Republic and 2004 in Germany). Considering that PLIVA has over 1500 SAP licenses, a help desk, ABAB programmers, highly educated employees (18 employees are SAP consultants) and an organizational management for user support, all the conditions have been set for PLIVA to become a SAP Customer Competence Center (certification in progress), which would then reduce the costs of license maintenance on 20%.

In 2001, the PLIVA Information Department achieved USD 1 million in revenues. Information strategy stems from the strategic business plans, in which 2% of revenues are earmarked for information, and the IT Committee gives global initiatives and a strategic development direction. In addition to the plans to implement new ERP modules (SCM, CRM), PLIVA also plans in the near future to create a unique methodology for project management.

Q1. Analyze the case based on various aspects of ERP implementation.

Q2. What type of Implementation approach did the company adopt and why

Q3. What advantage and disadvantage the company had due to following such an approach.

Annexure-I

IMPORTANT QUESTIONS

Q. 1. ***What is an Enterprise?***

Ans. An Enterprise is a group of people with a common goal, which has certain resources at its disposal to achieve that goal. When used generically, an enterprise is defined as the aggregate of all functional elements participating in a business process improvement action, regardless of the organizational structure housing those functional elements. It is a complete business consisting of functions, divisions, or other components used to accomplish specific objectives and defined goals.

Q. 2. What is ERP?

Ans. ERP is an acronym for Enterprise Resource Planning, and signifies the techniques and concepts employed for integrated management of businesses as a whole from the viewpoint of the effective use of management resources to improve the efficiency of an enterprise.

Q. 3. What are the main misconceptions about ERP?

Ans. There are many misconceptions about ERP. The first is that ERP is a computer system. Even though computers and IT are integral parts of an ERP system, ERP is primarily an enterprise-wide system, which encompasses corporate mission, objectives, attitudes, beliefs, values, operating style and people who make the organization. The second misconception is that ERP is for manufacturing organizations alone. This assumption is basically due to the way in which ERP was historically developed from the methods of Material Requirement Planning (MRP) and Manufacturing Resource Planning (MRP II), which are relevant to manufacturing organizations. In the manufacturing industry, MRP became the fundamental concept of production management and control in the mid 1970s. At this stage BOM (Bill of Materials), was the prevailing trend. And this concept unfolded from order inventory management of materials to plant and personnel planning and distribution planning, which in turn became MRP-II. This method incorporated financial accounting, human resource management functions, distribution management functions and management accounting functions, and globally came to cover all areas of enterprise mainstay business. Eventually it began to be called ERP. But in reality, the concept of enterprise-wide planning of resources is not limited to any particular segment of industry.

Q. 4. What are ERP packages?

Ans. ERP packages are integrated (covering all business functions) software packages that support the ERP concepts. ERP software is designed to model and automate many of the basic processes of a company, from finance to the shop floor, with the goal of integrating information across the company and eliminating complex, expensive links between computer systems that were never meant to talk to each other.

Q. 5. Who are the main players in the ERP market?

Ans. The main players are SAP AG, PeopleSoft, Oracle, Baan, JD Edwards, QAD, Ramco, IFS, Data Works, and so on.

Q. 6. When do the ERP system's set of generic processes produce dramatic improvements?

Ans. ERP software is a mirror image of the major business processes of an organization, such as customer order fulfillment and manufacturing. Its success depends upon reach—a circumscribed ERP system isn't much better than the legacy system it replaces. In many cases, it is worse because the old code at least was written specifically for the company and the task. ERP system's set of generic processes produce the dramatic improvements They are capable of only when used to connect parts of an organization and integrate its various processes seamlessly.

Q. 7. What are the reasons for the explosive growth of the ERP market?

Ans. Some of the reasons for the tremendous growth of the ERP market are the following:

- They enable improved business performance by achieving: Cycle time reduction, Increased business agility, Inventory reduction, Order fulfillment improvement, etc.
- They support business growth requirements
- They help companies in supporting new products/product lines and new customers by meeting their global requirements, including multiple languages and currencies.
- ERP systems provide flexible, integrated, real-time decision support thus,

improving responsiveness across the organization and eliminating the limitations in legacy systems like century dating issues, fragmentation of data and processing, inflexibility to change, insupportable technologies, etc.

- ERP packages can now be afforded by even small and medium sized businesses and offer increased functionality at a reasonable cost, support client server/open systems technologies and support vertical market solutions.

Q. 8. What are the direct benefits of ERP systems?

Ans. The following are some of the direct benefits of an ERP system:

- Business Integration
- Flexibility
- Better Analysis and Planning Capabilities
- Use of Latest Technology

Q. 9. What is Business Integration and how do the ERP systems achieve it?

Ans. The reason why ERP packages are referred to as being integrated, is the automatic data updation (automatic data exchange among applications) that takes place between related business components. Since conventional company information systems were aimed at the optimization of independent business functions in business units, almost all were weak in terms of the communication and integration of information that transcended the different business functions. In the case of large companies in particular, the timing of system construction and directives differs for each product and department/function and sometimes, they are disconnected. For this reason, it has become an obstacle in the shift to new product and business classification. In the case of ERP packages, the data of related business functions is also automatically updated at the time a transaction occurs. For this reason, one is able to grasp business details in real time, and carry out various types of management decisions in a timely manner, based on that information.

Q. 10. Why is it said that ERP systems are flexible?

Ans. One of the advantages of ERP packages is their flexibility. Different languages, currencies, accounting standards and so on can be covered in one system, and functions that comprehensively manage multiple locations of a company can be packaged and can be implemented automatically. To cope with company globalisation and system unification, this flexibility is essential, and one can say that it has major advantages, not simply for development and maintenance, but also in terms of management.

Q. 11. What are the factors that are critical for the success of the ERP implementation?

Ans. The factors that are important for the success of any ERP implementation are:

- Selection of the right package
- Commitment of top management
- Participation and dedication of the system's future users . Backing, support and cooperation of the IS/IT personnel
- Development of interfaces with current operational systems *and* with those under development
- Effort of consultants, who have respect for the company's Know-how and work culture
- Spirit and collaboration on the part of all.

Q. 12. How do conventional application packages and ERP packages differ?

Ans. First, the ERP packages cannot only have individual business functions such as accounts and inventory, but also the entire range of main business functions necessary for the company's operations.

The second difference is that ERP packages are targeted at everything from small businesses to the largest organizations, and that they can be composed of a highly flexible decentralized database and an information system cluster linked by a network.

The third difference is global adaptation, represented by ERP packages' multi-lingual and multi-currency capacity. In the present day, when companies, irrespective of their size and market share, are manufacturing and selling in various areas of the world, the globalization of management platforms is being hastened, along with the global adaptation of enterprise information systems.

Q. 13. What are the limitations of ERP?

Ans. ERP systems have three significant limitations:

1. Managers cannot generate custom reports or queries without help from a programmer and this inhibits them from obtaining information quickly, so that they can act on it for competitive advantage.

2. ERP systems provide current status only, such as open orders. Managers often need to look past the current status, to find trends and patterns that aid better decision-making.
3. The data in the ERP application is not integrated with other enterprise or division systems and does not include external intelligence.

Q. 14. Why are companies opting- for ERP systems?

Ans. Most companies are not satisfied with their current systems. On an average, their systems were developed over a decade ago. In spite of being chronologically recent, these systems are now a part of the distant past, once we take into account the complexities and the requirements imposed upon businesses by today's global market. Moreover, the role of information technology in business has also changed. The role of technology has evolved from simply a supporting operation to become an integral part of the business. As a result, software vendors developed sophisticated, all-encompassing and integrated software packages to address the needs of modern business. Companies find these packages to be feasible solutions to their information needs and hence, the demand for ERP systems.

Q. 15. Why can't the companies develop their own ERP packages?

Ans. Developing an ERP package is a very complex and time-consuming process, which needs a lot of skilled manpower and other resources. Many companies have personnel in their IT/IS departments, who can absorb the necessary knowledge and who have experience in developing sophisticated systems. The problem is that such specialised computer work is not the main business of these companies. The companies should be directing all their available resources into improving their own products or services, so that they can remain competitive, better serve their customers and continue to grow. Since designing and implementing integrated software packages is not the business of most companies, or a focus of their executives, the systems that their in-house team comes up with, will never equal in quality, scope, functionality or technology those systems which are created by software firms whose business this is. These software firms (ERP vendors) can produce sophisticated packages and provide their clients with products that allow them to maintain a focus on their own chief activities, thus improving revenues, profits and shareholder returns.

Q. 16. If developing a package is not a good option, then what is the best option?

Ans. As we have seen, it is better for companies to concentrate on their business and leave the job of developing the software package to people who are in that business. But to get maximum benefit out of a packaged solution, the company personnel should participate fully during the implementation of the package. The company should plan the participation so that its people play an appropriate role in the implementation project and so that the company was enough experts in-house, once the implementation is over. The company should bring in the know-how and experience that will guarantee the best possible use of the acquired package.

Q. 17. What is BPR?

Ans. BPR or Business Process Reengineering is the fundamental rethinking and radical redesign of business processes to achieve dramatic improvements in critical, contemporary measures of performance such as cost, quality, service and speed.

Q. 18. How does BPR differ from other management techniques?

Ans. There are many management disciplines that try to improve the competitiveness of organizations by redesigning the business processes and culture. The redesign approach can be either continuous process improvement or large-scale innovation, and it may rely on the application of modern technology. While many management principles rely on small, incremental and continuous improvements, BPR believes in a radical rethinking and dramatic change on the enterprise-wide level.

Q. 19. Isn't BPR just a term for commonsense management?

Ans. No doubt, there is a lot of plain common sense contained in BPR. However, common sense is not common action. BPR is a disciplined, structured approach to integrate common sense management principles into visible changes and improvements. Commonsense alone, without a formal structure, is incomplete. The organization needs a methodology to integrate effort and create team accomplishment towards a common measurable goal.

Q. 20. Will BPR institutionalize improvement and cultural change?

Ans. There is never a simple solution, or an easy fix, when dealing with complex organizations or diversified missions. With commitment and discipline, BPR will force change and improvement throughout an organization. It is through a total workforce involvement, along with improvement successes, that the culture will undergo change and acceptance.

Q. 21. Will BPR take away the management responsibility and turn it over to the employees?

Ans. In a modern organization, the manager possesses both the responsibility and authority to get a job done. Authority can be delegated to subordinates to empower them, but responsibility can only be shared. When the subordinate is successful, the manager is successful. BPR pushes authority and responsibility to the point of decision and increases the probabilities for success for all. Even though not a directly playing participant, the coach of a team wins or loses with the players. The advantage is that the effort of a team working together, with a common purpose under a coach's general guidance, is always better than the efforts of individuals.

Q. 22. How can an organization minimize staff time required to get through a BPR project?

Ans. There are several ways to speed the BPR process and minimise the staff time required. A few are:

- Get the best-qualified persons to do the job
- Develop a clear scope for the project
- Restrict the size of the process for review

Though these methods will reduce the time required, they will also limit the gains and the full capability for integration within the organization. The time used in the BPR process will more than pay for itself with the gains in effectiveness and efficiency.

Q. 23. What is the incentive if there is no guarantee of assistance, like retraining, if an employee were to lose the job through BPR?

Ans. The results of a BPR project are rarely the total elimination of a meaningful activity or job position. Its major intent is to improve the flow and efficiency of the work processes. Though there is an outside possibility that some unnecessary jobs may be identified, it is more likely that these had already been identified and were likely to be reduced in any case. A BPR project not only identifies the weak areas, but also the important but unperformed work. The transition plan that moves the process from the old to the new, should provide for retraining employees, where necessary, to meet new work challenges or tasks. Though there is never a guarantee, it is likely that BPR will be the instrument of change for realigning the workforce along with the work.

Q. 24. Why can't we just let a consultant do BPR for us?

Ans. A consultant can assist the BPR effort by explaining and guiding the use of the methodology and by providing technical assistance, when necessary, for modeling, activity-based costing and other techniques. But, the consultant will never understand the underlying business and its environment as well as those who work in it. More importantly in-house staff will truly believe in a product that was created by their own hands, with the direct endorsement of the managers and leaders. A new process is created by those who know it best and who must live with the changes that are planned.

Q. 25. How is BPR connected to ERP?

Ans. BPR used to be a buzzword until a few years ago. BPR suggests radical changes to improve the competitiveness of a company and uses Information Technology as one of its most important tools. ERP packages integrate business processes, enable the seamless flow of information across departmental barriers and help in automating the business process and procedures. So, ERP is an ideal solution for the reengineering processes.

Q. 26. What is MIS?

Ans. MIS or Management Information System is a computer-based system that optimises the collection, collation, transfer and presentation of information throughout an organization through an integrated structure of databases and information flow.

Q. 27. What are the main differences between MIS and data processing (DP) systems?

Ans. The major differences between a management information system and a data processing system are:

- The integrated database of the MIS enables greater flexibility in meeting the information needs of the management.
- The MIS integrates the information flow between functional areas (accounting, marketing, manufacturing, etc.) whereas data processing systems tend to support a single functional area.
- MIS caters to the information needs of all levels of management whereas data processing systems focus on departmental-level support.

- Management's information needs are supported on a more timely basis with the MIS (with its on-line query capability) than with a data processing system.

Q. 28. What are the main characteristics of a management information system?

Ans. The main characteristics of a management information system are:

- The MIS supports the data processing functions of transaction handling and record keeping.
- A MIS uses an integrated database and supports a variety of functional areas.
- A MIS provides operational, tactical and strategic levels of the organization with timely, but for most part, structured information (ad-hoc query facility is not available).
- A MIS is flexible and can be adapted to the changing needs of the organization.

Q. 29. What is DSS?

Ans. A DSS (Decision Support System) is an information and planning system that provides the ability to interrogate computers on an ad-hoc basis, analyze information and predict the impact of decisions before they are made. DBMSs let you select data and derive information for reporting and analysis. Spreadsheets and modeling programs provide both analysis and 'what if?' planning. However, any single application that supports decision-making is not a DSS. A DSS is a cohesive and integrated set of programs that share data and information. An integrated DSS has a direct impact on the management's decision-making process and it can be a very cost-beneficial computer application.

Q. 30. How does a DSS help in better decision-making?

Ans. A DSS can help close the information gap and allow managers to improve the quality of their decisions. To do this, the DSS hardware and software employ the latest technological innovations, planning and forecasting models, 4th generation languages and even artificial intelligence. In many cases, a DSS facilitates the decision-making process, by helping the decision-makers to choose between alternatives. Some decision support systems can automatically rank the alternatives based on the criteria given by the decision-maker. A DSS also helps in removing the monotony and tedium of gathering and analyzing data.

Q. 31. What are the main characteristics of a DSS?

Ans. The main characteristics of a DSS are:

- A DSS is designed to address semi-structured and unstructured problems.
- The DSS mainly supports decision-making at the top management level.
- DSS is interactive, user-friendly and can be used by the decision maker with little or no assistance from a computer professional.
- DSS makes general-purpose models, simulation capabilities and other analytical tools available to the decision-maker.

Q. 32. How is a DSS different from a MIS?

Ans. A DSS does not replace the MIS; instead it supplements the MIS. There are distinct differences between them. A MIS emphasizes on planned reports on a variety of subjects; a DSS focuses on decision-making. A MIS is standard, scheduled, structured and routine; a DSS is quite unstructured and is available on request. A MIS is constrained by the organizational system; a DSS is immediate and user-friendly.

Q. 33. What is EIS?

Ans. EIS or Executive Information System is an information system that consolidates and summarizes are the ongoing transactions within an organization. It should provide management with all the information it requires, at all times, from internal as well as external sources. Executive decision-making also requires access to outside information from competitors, governmental regulations, trade groups, news gathering agencies, and so on. A high degree of uncertainty and a future orientation is involved in most executive decisions. A successful EIS is easy to use, is flexible and customizable and uses the latest technological innovations.

Q. 34. What is a Data Warehouse?

Ans. A data warehouse is a database designed to support decision-making in an organization. It is updated batch-wise and is structured for fast online queries and summaries for managers. Data warehouses can contain enormous amounts of data.

Q. 35. Why do you need a data warehouse?

Ans. As the amount of data in the operational database of an organization increases, the performance of the database begin to degrade. So, it is essential to separate the operational and non-operational data. Data archiving is not a good option because if the non-operational data is archived, there is little or no use for it. Especially since this data is a very valuable resource and is too precious to be kept in some archive. It is in this situation that a data warehouse comes in handy. The primary concept of data warehousing is that the data stored for business analysis can most effectively be accessed, by separating it from the data in the operational systems. The most important reason for separating data for business analysis, from the operational data, has always been the potential performance degradation the operational system that can result from the analysis processes. High performance and quick response time is almost universally critical for operational systems. The reasons to separate the operational data from analysis data have not significantly changed with the evolution of the data warehousing systems, except that now they are considered more formally during the data warehouse building process. Advances in technology and changes in the nature of business, have made many of the business analysis processes much m6re complex and sophisticated. In addition to producing standard reports, today's data warehousing systems support very sophisticated online analysis, including multi-dimensional analysis.

Q. 36. What is data mining and what are its advantages?

Ans. Data Mining is the process of identifying valid, novel, potentially useful, and ultimately comprehensible knowledge from databases that is used to make crucial business decisions. Modern data mining systems self learn from the previous history of the investigated system, formulating and testing hypotheses about the rules, which this system obeys. When concise and valuable knowledge about the system of interest had been discovered, it can and should be incorporated into some decision support system, so that it can help the manager to make wise and informed business decisions.

Q. 37. What is the need of automated and computerized data mining tools?

Ans. The main reason for automated computer systems for intelligent data analysis is the enormous volume of existing and newly appearing data that require processing. The amount of data accumulated each day by various businesses, scientific and governmental organizations around the world is daunting. Research organizations, academic institutions and commercial organizations create and store huge amounts of data each day. It becomes impossible for human analysts to cope with such overwhelming amounts of data.

Two other problems that surface when human analysts process data, are, the inadequacy of the human brain when searching for complex multifactor dependencies in the data and the lack of objectiveness in its analysis. A human expert is always a hostage of the previous experience of investigating other systems. Sometimes this helps, sometimes this hurts, but it is almost impossible to get rid of this fact.

Q. 38. What is OLAP?

Ans. OLAP or On-line Analytical Processing is a decision support software that allows the user to quickly analyze information that has been summarized into multidimensional views and hierarchies. For example, OLAP tools are used to perform trend analysis on sales and financial information. They can enable users to drill down into masses of sales statistics in order to isolate the products that are the most volatile. Simply put, OLAP describes a class of technologies that are designed for live ad-hoc data access and analysis. While transaction processing (OLTP) generally relies on relational databases, OLAP has become synonymous with multidimensional views of business data. These multidimensional views are supported by multidimensional database technology and provide the technical basis for the calculations and analysis required by Business Intelligence applications.

OLAP technology is being used in an increasingly wide range of applications. The most common are sales and marketing analysis; financial reporting and consolidation; and budgeting and planning. Increasingly however, OLAP is being used for applications such as product profitability and pricing analysis; activity based costing, manpower planning; quality analysis, in fact for any management system that requires a flexible, top down view of an organization.

Q. 38. What is a supply chain?

Ans. A supply chain is a network of facilities and distribution options that performs the functions of procurement of materials, transformation of these materials into intermediate and finished products, and the distribution of these finished products to customers.

Q. 40. What is supply chain management?

Ans. A supply chain is a collection of inter-dependent steps that, when followed, accomplish a certain objective, such as meeting customer requirements. Supply-chain management is a generic term that encompasses the coordination of order generation, order taking and offer fulfillment/distribution of products, services, or information. Numerous, independent firms and customers are involved in a supply chain (manufacturers and parts suppliers; parcel shippers, senders and receivers; wholesalers and retailers). The WWW and extranets (connected intranets) have shown a great potential in linking and managing these entities into a virtual organization. For over 20 years, EDI has been promising such revolutionary gains but has failed to extend its benefit to small and medium companies. The remarkable nature of electronic commerce is its power in enabling all types, and sizes, of firms to interact.

Q. 41. What are the benefits cf using the Internet for supply chain management?

Ans. Interoperable intranets make it easy for supply-chain partners to share and exchange information, and at the same time, the whole management process may be contracted to a third party instead of developing one's own applications and investing in separate systems. In this intermediated market, sophisticated logistics management and automated supply-chain management are available almost universally.

Q. 42. What are the different phases of the ERP implementation lifecycle?

Ans. The different phases of the ERP implementation are:

- Pre-evaluation Screening
- Package Evaluation
- Project Planning Phase
- Gap Analysis
- Reengineering
- Configuration
- Implementation Team Training
- Testing
- Going Live
- End user Training
- Post-implementation

Q. 43. Why is the pre-evaluation screening required?

Ans. There are hundreds of ERP vendors—of all sizes and shapes—all claiming to have the solution that is ideal for your company. Analyzing all the packages before reaching a decision is not a viable solution. It is also a very time consuming process. So it is better to limit the number of packages that are evaluated to less than 5. It is always better to do a thorough and detailed evaluation of a small number of packages, rather than doing a superficial analysis of dozens of packages. It is to identify these packages that we need the pre-evaluation screening.

Q. 44. What are the factors to be considered when selecting an ERP package?

Ans. When selecting an ERP package, the following factors should be considered:

- Functional fit with the company's business processes
- Degree of integration between the various components of the ERP system
- Flexibility and scalability
- Complexity
- User friendliness
- Quick implementation
- Ability to support multi-site planning and control
- Technology—client/server capabilities, database independence, security
- Availability of regular upgrades
- Amount of customization required
- Local support infrastructure
- Availability of reference sites
- Total costs, including cost of license, training, implementation, maintenance, customization and hardware requirements.

Q. 45. What is Gap analysis?

Ans. Gap analysis is a phase in the ERP implementation, where the organization tries to find out the gaps between the company's existing business practices and those supported by the ERP package. Put very simply, this is the process through which companies create a complete model of where they are now and where they are heading. The trick is to design a model, which both anticipates and covers any functional gaps. It has been estimated that even the best ERP package, custom tailored to a company's needs, meets only 80% of the company's functional requirements.

Q. 46. How are the 'gaps', found out during the gap analysis phase filled?

Ans. This can be done in different ways. One of the most affordable, but most difficult, solutions entails altering the business to 'fit' the ERP package. Another solution is that the company can simply agree to live without a particular function (the cheap but annoying solution). Other solutions include:

- Pinning your hopes on an upgrade (low cost but risky)
- Identifying a third-party product that might fill the gap (hopefully it also partners with the ERP packages, keeping interfacing to a minimum)
- Designing a custom program
- Altering the ERP source code, (the most expensive alternative; usually reserved for mission-critical installations)

Q. 47. Can the ERP software packages fit the business needs of the organizations well?

Ans. No package is perfect. You cannot get a package that covers each and every requirement of the company (a perfect fit). It is impossible to get a system that will perform, exactly as the company does business, but the aim should be to get the system that has the least number of differences. Due to globalization, there has been a significant amount of uniformity, standardization and simplification of the core business practices and processes across the world. Some of the technologies, such as EDI and EFT, function the same way across the globe and have the same set of standards and procedures. These developments permit the ERP vendors to develop a world-class software that can be profitably used by a corporation in Chennai as well as in New York. By spending huge amounts of money for research and for gaining an understanding of the business practices and processes used by thousands of corporations worldwide, the ERP software vendors bring in world-class practices to any company that implements the ERP software. Also, the big ERP vendors employ and retain thousands of software professionals who continuously improve their ERP software product. No individual end user company can afford such a large pool of software professionals. This is the secret for the success of ERP. But it is estimated that even the best ERP package, custom tailored to a company's needs, meets only 80% of the company's functional requirements. The remaining 20% has to be identified {during the gap analysis) and then, suitable solutions are implemented.

Q. 48. What is electronic commerce?

Ans. The term "electronic commerce" has evolved from electronic shopping to imply all aspects of business and market processes enabled by the Internet and the World Wide Web technologies. Electronic Commerce means doing business online or selling and buying products and services through Web storefronts.

Products being traded may be physical products such as used cars or services (e.g. arranging trips, online medical consultation and remote education). Increasingly, they include digital products such as news, audio and video, database, software and all types of knowledge-based products. It appears then that electronic commerce is similar to catalog shopping or home shopping on cable TV.

But electronic commerce is not limited to buying and selling products online. For example, a neighborhood store can open a Web store and find the world in its doorstep. But, along with customers, it will also find its suppliers, accountants, payment services, government agencies and competitors online. These online or digital partners will demand changes in the way we do business from production to consumption, and they will affect companies who might think that they are not part of electronic commerce. Along with online selling, electronic commerce will lead to significant changes in the way products are customized, distributed and exchanged and the way consumers search and bargain for products and services and consume them.

In short, the success of electronic commerce revolution lies in the way it effects processes. Process-oriented definition of electronic commerce offers a broader view of what it is. Within-business processes (e.g. manufacturing, inventorying, corporate financial management, operation) and business-to-business processes (e.g. supply-chain management, bidding) are affected by the same technology and network as are business-to-consumer processes. Even government functions, education, social and political processes undergo changes.

Q. 49. Why is the Internet different from other computer and network technologies?

Ans. Two things make the Internet quite different from any other existing communications media. Unlike broadcasting media, the Internet (1) allows two-way-communications and (2) is built around open standards. A two-way communication means targeting audience and the possibility of feedback. Broadcasting sends out messages to "no one in particular" and without knowing quite who has gotten the message. An open standard (e.g. TCP/IP) means interoperability and the advantage of a large market and the possibility of integrating one product or process with another.

Q. 50. What is Intranet?

Ans. There is no technical difference between the Internet and the intranet, except that not everybody is allowed to connect to an intranet. Intranet is an application of the Internet technology to a closed network. It provides a relatively cost efficient way to connect and manage corporate networks and distributed information. Intranet uses Internet-derived communication protocols (TCP/IP), networking (IP network) and user interface (Web browsers, e-mails etc.). The surprising speed with which intranets have grown among corporate users, demonstrates the strength of the Internet networking. Several surveys contend that corporate intranet expenditure far out-paces the level of spending on consumer-oriented Web businesses (Web stores). The compatibility of corporate intranets with the Internet will be a significant factor in the digital economy. In a sense, producer and seller information is readily accessible by outsiders, making it easy to manage and disseminate information to consumers.

Q. 51. What is the difference between Intranet and Extranet?

Ans. Intranets and extranets have become *en vogue*. Intranets and extranets share the common protocol (TCP/IP) and Web technologies with the Internet. Intranet is a closed, business-wide network, but it uses open standards such as TCP/IP, instead of proprietary protocols traditionally used for LANs (local area networks, usually hard-wired) and WANs (wide area networks, usually LANs connected by cable, telephone and wireless networks). Extranet is a private WAN running on public protocols. That is, an extranet is a virtual private network among private parties based on open network and protocols. To assure security and privacy, an extranet relies on secured channels using tunneling protocols and digital ID.

Q. 52. What are enabling technologies?

Ans. The electronic marketplace is where information-age commodities (digital, knowledge-based products) are produced, exchanged and consumed. For the market to function, it requires substantial investments in market infrastructure that is capable of supporting transactions efficiently. The market infrastructure includes telecommunications networks (telephone, cable, wireless, etc.) that provide communication and delivery services. Another key component is that of interface devices and technologies, such as computer hardware, software and digital appliances. Network and computer technologies, in turn, enable various electronic commerce applications and other support services such as electronic payment systems. In this sense, networks and computers are enabling technologies of electronic commerce. Enabling technologies will change and improve: messages have been delivered by person, postal service, telephone, fax, and now by e-mail. Transportation and product delivery systems have been innovated over time. Just as likely, today's Internet and computing platforms will change. But these changes will not affect the fundamental nature of the digital economy. The electronic commerce revolution happened on the Internet because of its advantages such as open, distributed networking. Although technologies will determine the boundary of what processes can be implemented at a given time, it is the process we find useful that will shape the future of these technologies and the economy.

Q. 53. What is Convergence?

Ans. Both telecommunications networks and computer technologies are heading toward 'convergence'. In short, the convergence is a process that allows hitherto incompatible devices to talk to each other (interoperable), products to be interchangeable and processes to be integrated. The underlying impetus for convergence is the digital technologies or digitization. Its effect is much wider than the simple network convergence that we are aware of today.

- ***Product Convergence:*** Today, digital products include voice signals, TV programmes, musical CDs, videos, books, magazines, news and all types of paper-based information, database, computer software and games. Room and access keys are digital, and stored on a smart card; IDs and personal information are digital; and money is digital. All these digital products are essentially made up of ones and zeros (the on-and-off dual states of an electronic charge), capable of being transported via a telecommunications network.
- ***Network (Infrastructure) Convergence:*** Telephone, coaxial cable, broadcast, satellite and wireless networks are all capable of sending and receiving the same digital signals. When a telephone network is busy, one can re-direct the voice to cable or wireless networks.
- ***Market Convergence:*** Suddenly, several regulated monopolies are facing potential competition from those who used to be in different markets: telephone companies and cable TV operators are potential competitors. Internet service providers and TV broadcasters may be fighting for Internet access. The convergence in products and networks has resulted in the breakdown of old market boundaries, in addition to the lowering of geographical market

boundaries. (Of course, this potential competition will become real, only if these firms do indeed compete. Another type of convergence, i.e. mergers, or artificial market boundaries, will sustain monopoly status.)

- ***Process Convergence:*** We use process convergence in the sense of 'integration' where different processes (or phases in a value chain) are integrated into a seamless process. For example, online advertising gets an immediate feedback from its recipients, which is then used to modify production process (customizations). In broadcasting, advertising is almost separated from market research or any other business processes.

The convergence brings about new opportunities as well as uncertainties. As products are digitized, they acquire new characteristics which increase their appeal. For example, a CD-ROM version of an encyclopedia provides search and link capabilities far exceeding the cross-indexing features provided by book versions. New products mean new uses, new customers and new ways of doing business. Many focus on the opportunity to expand their business, but the novelty also creates uncertainty. For example, as the telecommunications infrastructure converges, traditional boundaries among telephone companies, cable operators and satellite operators become unclear. These companies are experimenting with video-on-demand services, interactive television, cable modems, online shopping, video dial-tone, etc. to gauge consumer response and future profitability in their widening playing field. Not knowing consumer demand and competitors' strategies, however, they are hesitant to plunge into the unknown. On the other hand, Bill Gates of Microsoft, Craig McCaw, who founded McCaw Cellular Communications, and other investors are willing to take a risk in the future of converging infrastructure. Their enterprise is called Teledesic Corp., which will invest almost $ 10 billion to place 840 low earth-orbiting satellites around the earth. The plan is to offer broadband connection, broadcasting, video conferencing and other telecommunications services worldwide through its satellite network. The project's possible payoffs may be as large as the size of necessary investments.

Q. 54. What is EDI?

Ans. EDI or Electronic Data Interchange is the electronic communication of transactions between organizations, such as orders, confirmations and invoices. Independent service organizations provide EDI services that enable users to interconnect with another organization's network, regardless of the type of equipment used.

Q. 55. What is EDIFACT?

Ans. EDIFACT or Electronic Data Interchange For Administration Commerce and Transport is an ISO standard for EDI that is proposed to supersede both X12 and Tradacoms standards to become the worldwide standard.

Q. 56. What's new with today's EDI?

Ans. Traditional electronic data interchange (EDI) is an automated system of business-to-business data exchange. Two primary areas of EDI are data interchange (for orders, invoices) and electronic funds transfer (EFT) used among banks, which have a high volume in a relatively small number of data items, and long-term relationship. Setting up an EDI is expensive only large firms can justify investing in it. Security-wise, EDI offers robust transactions compared to the Internet, since EDI runs on closed, private value added networks (VANs). But for that reason, the number of trading partners is always limited to those who are connected to these VANs. An open EDI is a more flexible EDI, which can carry more types of data (including graphics) and is cost effective for short-term interactions. New standards for forms and communications are necessary to support open data interchanges. The cost advantage of the Internet will cause much of the existing EDI traffic to move into Internet-based EDI/VAN or secure 'extranets' that connect business sites via private communication channels ('tunnels'). Private VAN service providers themselves, will play a role in the Internet traffic business. *But with EDI on the Internet, EDI-enabled transactions and business processes will be available to and used by firms who couldn't afford to invest in EDI/VAN networks.* More EDI-like services will be offered more widely, which may finally bring about a 'paperless' business that EDI-pioneers promised two decades ago.

Q. 57. Why is top management support essential for the success of ERP?

Ans. Any improvement that involves change will face resistance from all the employees. It is human nature to resist change. This resistance can be due to ignorance about the new system and its advantages, fear of unemployment and fear of new technology (fear of obsolescence), and so on. This is true for every effort that includes change; it is not limited to ERP implementation; it is the case with any new technology. To overcome the resistance at such a massive scale, the ERP implementation team needs top management support and commitment. It is the top management that should give assurance to the employees that their jobs are not endangered, that the new system is not a threat, but a solution to become competitive and remain in business. It is the top management that has to devise plans for relocating the employees when-ever that need arises, because an ERP implementation will involve a considerable amount of organizational restructuring. Also, when employees know that the top management is committed to and is firmly behind the ERP implementation, the chances of resistance are less. To get the necessary resources, the ERP teams needs to have some firepower, and for that it is better that the ERP implementation efforts are headed by somebody high up in the corporate ladder, like the CIO or COO, who have the necessary authority and influence to get things done.

Q. 58. What is the importance of end-user training?

Ans. The success or failure of an ERP system rests with how the actual users use it. Even the most successfully implemented ERP systems fail to deliver the dramatic performance improvements that it has promised due to lack of end-user cooperation. ERP systems will change the job descriptions and functions of many employees. People who were used for recording information (like an order entry clerk) are overnight turned into decision-makers, whose actions have far reaching consequences throughout the organizations. Since ERP is automated and is integrated, an action by an employee in the purchasing department can have its effect felt in many other departments like manufacturing, stores, sales and distribution, finance and so on. Many employees are hesitant to make this job shift which involves additional responsibilities. The employees also feel that since many procedures are getting automated, their jobs are at stake. So, it is important that even before the actual ERP implementation starts, an awareness program for the employees explaining the details of the new system and clearing their doubts and misconceptions is conducted. It is also important to reassure them that ERP is not a system to replace employees. The management should explain to the people, the potential benefits of the new system and the changes in the organizational structure and job profiles. The employees should also be given enough training to make a successful transformation to their new jobs. Many ERP systems fail, because the end-user training was not properly planned and implemented.

Q. 59. What is business modeling?

Ans. Business modeling is the method of diagrammatically representing the business as a large system showing the interconnections and business subsystems and processes of the business. It is a means to map the organizations processes and visualise it in a graphical manner. This helps in communication, clarification and documentation of the "AS IS" and "TO BE" processes.

Q. 60. Is ERP specific to manufacturing industries?

Ans. Even though the ERP systems evolved from the manufacturing systems like MRP and MRP-II as the market matured, the ERP vendors added additional functionality and features to their ERP packages so that they could cater to the need of any industry. Now, ERP systems are not specific to manufacturing industries, but are available to all industries.

Q. 61. What are the different approaches of ERP implementation?

Ans. There are mainly three different approaches to ERP implementation—the 'big bang' approach, location-wise and module-wise implementation. In the big bang approach, the organization decides to implement all relevant modules at the same time. This has the advantage of getting the full benefit of the integrated software across all functions of the organization. However, there is a risk of the implementation getting out of control. In 'Location-wise' implementation, the organization chooses a specific location, say. the head office, one of the new plants, etc. In 'module-wise' implementation. Individual modules are taken up for implementation in a phased manner, depending on the criticality of applications. Once a module is taken up for implementation, it can be implemented across all locations or in just one location.

Q. 62. What is an integrated data model?

Ans. The most important part in any ERP project is the creation of an integrated data model (IDM). The ERP package should provide true integration of the entire systems of the enterprise and should make the information available to all who need it. The integrated data model, and the enterprise-wide database created using it, should reflect the transactions that are taking place in the organization in real time.

Q. 63. What are some of the tangible benefits of ERP?

Ans. Some of the tangible benefits of ERP are lead time reduction, on-time delivery/shipments, increased business volumes, lower inventory levels, increased inventory turnover, reduction in cycle time, reduction in work-in-progress, improved quality and so on.

Q. 64. What are some of the intangible benefits of ERP?

Ans. The intangible benefits include improved customer satisfaction, better integration with vendor, increased flexibility, reduction in quality costs, better capacity utilization, improved decision-making ability and so on.

Q. 65. Is ERP implementation costly?

Ans. The cost of ERP implementation used to be very high, thus making ERP only available to very big organizations. But this cost is gradually coming down, so that even medium-sized and small businesses can go for it. The reasons for this are the fierce competition in the ERP market, saturation of high-end market segments, and so on.

Q. 66. Will there be an increase in productivity after the ERP implementation?

Ans. The success of an ERP implementation depends on a lot of factors, like having the right package, having the right implementation methodology and cooperation of the end-users. Successful ERP implementations will definitely improve productivity. The experience in other countries show that productivity levels have grown 3-4 times after implementing the ERP system. In India it is too early to have any real statistics on this matter, but many companies have claimed dramatic improvements in productivity.

Q. 67. What is the difference between MRP/MRP-II and ERP?

Ans. While MRP and MRP-II are systems that address the requirements of a manufacturing setup, ERP addresses the information needs and requirements of the entire enterprise. The focus of ERP has not only been on addressing the current requirements of the organization, but also on providing the opportunity for continually improving and refining the business processes. Since the system is integrated, the redundant data and processes are eliminated. The ERP system is integrated as well as automated, thus automating the business procedures on an enterprise level. For example, an order entered by an order entry clerk in the purchase department will trigger a lot of actions in many other departments, like sales and distribution, finance, manufacturing and so on.

Q. 68. What is BE?

Ans. BE or Business Engineering revolves around information technology and continuous change. It is the constant refinement of an organization's changing needs. It is the re-thinking of business processes to improve the speed, quality and output of materials or services.

Q. 69. What are the benefits of BE?

Ans. BE makes the companies competitive, by making them more customer-focused and responsive to changes in the marketplace. It achieves these results by reshaping the corporate structures around business processes. BE implements change not by the complete automation of business but rather by the redefinition of the company tasks in holistic or process-oriented terms. Only companies with innovative staff, products and services as well as short development cycles, will be able to remain competitive in today's business world. By maximizing individual and team creativity and by emphasizing a process-oriented approach, BE enables a company to realize these goals.

Q. 70. What is Extended ERP?

Ans. Extended ERP is a set of enterprise modeling tools for effective implementation. This is a concept promoted by the Baan company for rapid, flexible and quality implementation of ERP systems. These implementation tools have been developed on the **basic premise that the customer should be able to implement ERP solutions with** minimum consultancy.

Q. 71. Will the workload of the employee's decrease after the ERP implementation?

Ans. An ERP package is expected to improve the flow of information and formalise, integrate and automate all the business processes and workflow that exist in an organization. Many users expect their workload to reduce after an ERP implementation; but this may not always happen. The important thing to understand is that the ERP package is an enabling tool to help the users do their job better and faster.

Q. 72. Will ERP systems eliminate clerical jobs? If yes, what should those employees do?

Ans. ERP packages automate the business processes through the use of technology. This can eliminate the jobs of many staff members, whose function is to record, control, calculate, compare, file or prepare reports. But this same trend (the trend of automation) creates windows of opportunity for professionals, as they can liberate themselves from the way things are still done in most companies. They can start preparing themselves to become highly valued individuals in a new work environment that will demand completely new functions; in which the use of technology at hand, relationships with clients and suppliers, the generation of added value to the company's products, the constant updating of know-how, and a multidisciplinary approach will become the differentiating factors in evaluating leaders.

Q. 73. What are the direct benefits of an ERP implementation?

Ans. The direct advantages include improved efficiency, reduced cycle time, reduced lead-limes, improved capacity and resource utilisation, information integration for better decision-making, faster response time to customer queries, etc.

Q. 74. What are the indirect benefits of an ERP implementation?

Ans. The indirect benefits include better corporate image, improved customer goodwill, customer satisfaction, reduced quality costs, improved information accuracy, better decision-making capability, and so on.

Q. 75. What is lead-time?

Ans. The elapsed time between placing an order and receiving it is known as the lead-time.

Q. 76. What is cycle time?

Ans. Cycle time is the time between receipt of the order and delivery of the product.

Q. 77. How do you measure the degree of customer satisfaction?

Ans. Assessment of the degree of satisfaction is usually made on at least three measures. They are:

- Whether the product or service includes the features that are most important to the customer
- Whether the company can respond to the customers' demands in a timely manner, a criterion that is especially important for custom products and services
- Whether the product or service is free of defects and performs as expected

Q. 78. What is product flexibility?

Ans. Product flexibility is the ability of the operation to efficiently produce highly customized and unique products.

Q. 79. What are quality-related costs?

Ans. The quality-related costs are classified into the following four categories:

- Internal failure costs (costs of scrap, rework, re-inspection and low production yields for non-conforming items that are detected before they leave the company)

- External failure costs (warranty claims, repairs and service costs that result when the failure is detected in the market place)
- Appraisal costs (cost of inspecting upon arrival, during manufacture, in laboratory tests and by outside inspectors)
- Prevention costs (design and development of new quality equipment, evaluation costs of a new product or service, training of quality personnel).

Q. 80. What is an information system?

Ans. An information system is an open, purposive system that produces information using the 'input-process-output' cycle.

Q. 81. What are the elements of an information system?

Ans. The minimal information system consists of three elements—people, procedures and data.

Q. 82. What is a computerized information system?

Ans. A computerized information system is an organized combination of people, hardware, software, communications networks and data resources that collects, collates, transforms and disseminates in an organization.

Q. 83. What is the function of MIS?

Ans. MIS produces information products that support many of the day-to-day decision-making needs of the management.

Q. 84. What are the drawbacks of the traditional information systems?

Ans. The traditional information systems have two major disadvantages. One, the people in one department do not have any information about what is happening in the other departments. May be at the top management level, the summary reports are being circulated to other departments also, but these summary reports often fail in capturing the real picture. The second drawback is that these systems give only that information, which they were designed to produce at the time they were built. Suppose a manager wants to know some information, which is not in the reports, then these systems are of no help.

Q. 85. What is a Business model?

Ans. Business model is a representation of the business as one large system showing the interconnections and interdependencies of the various subsystems and business processes.

Q. 86. What is the future of the ERP market?

Ans. According to AMR Research, Inc. the leading industry and market analysis firm specializing in enterprise applications and enabling technologies, the Enterprise Resource Planning (ERP) software market will grow at a compound annual growth rate of 37 per cent over the next five years. According to the firm's Enterprise Resource Planning Software Report, 1997-2002, total company revenue will top $ 52 billion by the year 2002.

Q.87. Who are called the 'Big 5' in the ERP market?

Ans. The Big 5 are SAP AG, PeopleSoft, Oracle Corporation, Baan Company and JD Edwards.

Q. 88. Who is the leader in the ERP market and what are its products?

Ans. SAP AG is the market leader and its ERP products are SAP R/2 for the mainframe environment and SAP R/3 for the client/server environment.

Q. 89. What are the factors that are attributed for the growth in the ERP market?

Ans. The AMR group attributes the continued growth to these three primary-factors:

- ERP vendors are continuing to expand market presence by offering new applications such as supply chain management, sales force automation, customer support and human resources.
- To sustain their rapid growth, ERP vendors will try to sell more licenses into their installed base. Currently, ERP vendors have a 10-20 per cent penetration (i.e. percentage of total employees currently using the ERP system). This will grow to 40-60 per cent within the next five years.
- While ERP originated in the manufacturing market, ERP usage has spread to nearly every type of enterprise including retail, utilities, the public sector and healthcare organizations. Most will purchase new ERP systems over the next five years, often for the first time.

Q. 90. Name some of the ERP products and their manufacturers?

Ans. SAP R/3 by SAP, PeopleSoft by PeopleSoft, One World by JD Edwards, Oracle Applications by Oracle, Bann by Bann Company, Marsha! by Ramco, MFG/PRO by QAD, BPCS by SSA and so on.

Q. 91. What are the major modules in an ERP system?

Ans. The major modules include Finance, Manufacturing, Materials Management, Sales and Distribution, Plant Maintenance, Quality Management, Logistics Management, and so on.

Q. 92. Who are ERP vendors?

Ans. Vendors are the people who have developed the ERP packages. They are the people who have invested a huge amount of time and effort in research and development, to create the packaged solutions.

Q. 93. Who are business consultants?

Ans. Business consultants are professionals, who specialize in developing techniques and methodologies for dealing with the implementation and the various problems that crop up during the implementation. They are experts in the administration, management and control of these types of projects. Each of them will have many man-years of implementation experience with various industries and would have time-tested methodologies and business practices that will ensure a successful implementation. They will be good at all phases of the implementation life-cycle, right from package evaluation to end-user training.

Q. 94. Why is not a good idea to implement the ERP system using an in-house team?

Ans. To successfully set up and implement an ERP package, which will function perfectly, is not an easy task. One cannot go in for a trial-and-error method of implementation strategy due to the huge amount of investments involved. The consequences of a failed ERP implementation can be quite catastrophic. It might put the organization out of business. Also, the ERP implementation process cannot go on for a long time. It has to be completed within a reasonable time period.

To successfully carry out the implementation within a reasonable timeframe, the in-house people, who are designated to do the job, should possess a certain amount of knowledge and skills. To start with, the company should have many people who are experts with the ERP package and with the technical issues. Implementing the ERP software means assigning the optimum values to the various parameters and variable elements of the system. So, the company needs experienced professionals for a successful implementation, but once the implementation is over, the company needs only a handful of experts to run the system successfully. So, it is better to get the help of implementation experts from outside.

Q. 95. Who are end-users and why are they important?

Ans. End-users are the people who will be using the ERP system once it is in place. These are the people who were doing the functions that are being automated or computerised by the ERP system. With the implementation of the ERP system, the old job descriptions will change and the nature of the job will also undergo a drastic transformation. It is human nature to resist change. When we are talking about implementing an ERP system, we are talking about change on a very massive scale. So, there will be a fear of the system replacing existing jobs, as many functions will be automated. Also, people might be afraid of the amount of training they would have to undergo and the learning they would have to do to use the new system. Job profiles will change, job responsibilities will undergo drastic alterations and people will be forced to develop new skill sets. If these fears are not addressed and alleviated well in advance, then it will be asking for trouble. It should be worth noting the fact that while the ERP systems eliminate many existing jobs, it creates many new ones—ones with more responsibilities and value addition. It is easy to see that the automation of the business processes through technology, can eliminate the jobs of many employees whose function is to record, control, calculate, analyse, file or prepare reports. But it must be pointed out to the employees that the same automation creates many -more opportunities for them because they can get away from the monotonous clerical work and transform themselves into highly valued individuals, in a new and challenging work environment using the most modern technology. If the company can succeed in making its employees accept this fact and assist them in making the transformation (by giving them training), then the major (and most critical) obstacle in the path of an ERP implementation is solved. Without the support and cooperation of the end-users, no ERP implementation will succeed.

REFERENCES

1. Alexis Leon, Enterprise resource planning, Tata McGraw Hill Publishing Co., Ltd, New Delhi-1999.

2. Alexis Leon, ERP- Demystified, Tata McGraw Hill Publishing Co. Ltd. New Delhi-2002

3. Computer World(2001) ERP Trends, September-October.

4. Martin M.H.(1998)" An ERP Strategy" Fortune,2 February, p.95-97.

5. Noori H & Mavaddat F.,1998,"Enterprise integration issues and methods", International Journal of production Research,36(8),2093-2108.

6. Stater, D.,1999, An ERP package for you and you, CIO magazine Feb 15, 1999.

7. Sudhakar ram, " Enterprise Resource Planning", Director and Master ltd.

8. Polly Schneider, wanted ERP People Skills, CIO magazine, March 1, 1999.

9. Austin, R.D.and Nolan, R.L.(1998), " Manage ERP Initiatives as New Ventures, Not IT Projects",Working Paper, Boston, Harvard Business School:pp.127.

10. Dr. Subodh Kesharwani, ERP Systems, Application, Experiences& Upsurge, Pragati Prakashan.

11. Koch, C.(2001), 'BPR and ERP : realizing a vision of process with IT', Business process management Journal, vol.7, number3,258-265.

12. Light Ben (2000) ERP & Best of Breed: A Competitive analysis, Business process management, Journal vol.7 Number3 pp 216-224.

13. Light Ben (2000) ERP & Best of Breed: A Competitive analysis, Business process management, Journal vol.7 Number3 pp 216-224.

14. Teng James, Varun Grover & Kirk Fieldler, "Re-Designing Business Process Using Information Technology," Long Range Planning, vol.27, Number1, 1994.

15. "Data Mine Fields," PC week, vol., Number12(1996),17-20.

16. IEEE Intelligent Systems, special issues on Data Mining II, March /April 2000.

17. IEEE Intelligent Systems, special issues on Data Mining II, November/ December 2000.

18. IEEE Computer Special Issue on Data Mining, Vol.32, Number 8, August 1999.

19. Sidney Hill, Jr., "How To Be A Trendsetter: Dassault And IBM PLM Customers Swap Tales From The PLM Front", retrieved on March 28, 2008.

20. http://www.methodfocus.com/exped.htm

21. http://www.datawarehouse-institute.htm

22. http://www.datawarehouse.itoolbox.htm

23. Bird,Jane,"Data in Knowledgeout", Management Today,(September,1996),70-72.

24. http://erp.itoolbox.com/wp/hp3.asp?i=3121dated 08-01-2005.

25. http://www.ascet.com/documents.asp?grlD=138&d_ID=270.

26. E_Supply Chain, Charles.C. Poirer&Michael J. Bauer, Berett_Koehler Publishers Inc.2000, pp 116-124.

27. Administering SAP R/3 : Sd Sales and Distribution Module Asap world consultancy.

28. Administering SAP R/3 : Fi_ Finance & Co_Control Module ASap world Consultancy

29. Administering SAP R/3 : Mm_material management module jonathan blane

30. Zrimsek,B.and Genovese, Y.(2000), The 2000 ERP market –year in review, Gartner.

31. http://www.computerworld.com/cwi/printer_friendly_version/0,1212,NAV47_ST034

32. Processes.Kluwer Academic, Boston

33. Umble,E.Ji(2002) Avoiding ERP IMplemeentation Failure, Industrial Management February

34. F. Roberts Jacobs & D. Clay Whybark (2003) Why ERP? A primer on SAP implementation, New York, Mc Graw Hill

35. Jackson, M.A.;" System Development ;, Prentice Hall, New Jersey ; 1983.

36. Wirfs_Brock, R., Wilkerson, B, Wiener, L.; Designing Object _ oriented Software ; Prentice Hall.

37. Bancroft Nancy, Honning Seip & Andrea Sprengel,Implementing SAP R/3, Manning Publications Co. 2nd Edition 1998.

38. E-Business and ERP, Grant Norris, James R. Hurley, Kenneth M. Hartley, John Dunleavy John Wiley & Sons, Inc., 2000.

39. Garrett Dave," Internet Versus Intranet Development", DM Review, VOL.7, NUMBER4, Apirl 1997,pp.40-43.

40. http://www.iiitb.ac.in/papers/critical .html

41. Chen,II, Planning for ERP, Management journal, vol.7,number5,374-386.

42. Davenport J.H., Mission Critical, Hardvard Business School Press

43. Aladwani, Change management strategies for successful ERP implementation: Business process management journal, vol.7,n0.3, 266-275.

44. http://www.fcm.com

45. http://www.isi.upc.es

46. Hallows,J.,Information systems project management, Amacom, Tokyo, pp.283.

47. Haberman, F. and Scheer, A.W., "Making ERP a Success", ACM.

48. Callaway, Erin." A New Dawn for ERP Suppliers", Management Automation, 9/2000.

49. Callaway, Erin." ERP:Tiers one & Two", Management Automation, 6/2000.

50. Bond B. et al, ERP is Dead Long Live ERP II, Gartner Group, 2000.

51. Zrimsek, B.et al(2001), Estimating the time & cost of ERP and ERPII projects:A10-step process, Gartner.

52. http://en.wikipedia.org/wiki/Software_development_process

53. Enterprise Resource Planning (ERP) - Impact Of The Internet On Erp Systems, http://ecommerce.hostip.info/pages/418/Enterprise-Resource-Planning-ERP-IMPACT-INTERNET-ON-ERP-SYSTEMS.html

54. Bosilj Vukšić, V. & Spremić, M. (2005). ERP system Implementation and Business Process Change: Case Study of a Pharmaceutical Company, Journal of Computing and Information Technology - CIT 13, No. 1., 11–24.